365 DAYS OF
DIY

White Lemon

BOOK NAME

―――――§―――――

by White Lemon

Copyright © White Lemon 2016

This book is licensed for your personal enjoyment only. This book may not be re-sold or given away to other people. If you would like to share this book with another person, please purchase an additional copy for each recipient. If you're reading this book and did not purchase it, or it was not purchased for your enjoyment only, then please return to your favorite retailer and purchase your own copy. Thank you for respecting the hard work of this author, White Lemon: whitelemon_diy@yahoo.com

See more books by White Lemon:
www.amazon.com/author/whitelemon

Disclaimer

No part of this publication may be reproduced in any form or by any means, including printing, photocopying, or otherwise without prior written permission of the copyright holder. If you would like to use material from the book (other than just simply for reviewing the book), prior permission must be obtained by contacting the author.

ISBN-13: 978-1539929611

Contents

Introduction 1

Chapter 1: DIY Household Hacks and DIY Projects 3

1. Position old doorknobs in your bathroom to hang clothes and towels. 4
2. Create a bracelet holder on an older paper towel holder. 4
3. Hide your ugly thermostat behind a hinged painting. 5
4. Paint your walls with polka dots with an old laundry basket. 5
5. Create beautiful shelves with your old dresser drawers. 5
6. Use a wine rack for a kitchen towel holder. 6
7. Hang your ironing board on two coat hangers. 6
8. Use a shoe organizer to organize your snacks in the pantry! 6
9. Use an old '90s CD tower for your bathroom organization. 7
10. Pour your cleaning solution or laundry detergent into a drink dispenser. 7
11. Place magazine racks in your pantry to store your cans. 7
12. Keep a bit of extra room paint in a small baby food jar, for easy touch-ups. 8
13. Better spare key hiding than ever before. 8
14. Place another shower curtain rod in your shower for better storage opportunities. ... 8
15. Use dry erase marker on your bathroom mirror for helpful hints and reminders. 9
16. Place a phone book in the back of deep storage spaces to keep track of everything. ... 9
17. Screw foam noodles into the walls of your garage. 9
18. Create a eucalyptus fragrance explosion in your shower. 10
19. Store cords on plastic hangers. 10
20. Hide your Internet router with fake books. 10
21. Remove the indentations from your carpet with ice cubes. 11
22. Keep your door open with a rubber band. 11
23. Organize your plastic bags with a Kleenex box. 12
24. Plop a ball of aluminum foil into your dryer for a better dryer sheet! 12
25. Remove pet hair from your carpet with a window squeegee. 12
26. Position your storage bag and garbage bag cardboard containers in your pantry with thumbtacks. 13
27. Position Christmas lights in your closet for better lighting. 13
28. Position your shower hooks on your closet rod to make clothes accessible. 13
29. Position a magnetic strip of tape beneath your food or storage cabinets to place metal-topped spices beneath. 14
30. Place a letter organizer in your closet to organize flat shoes. 14
31. Place a Command hook on the other side of your baby's high chair for bib-hanging. 14
32. Disinfect Legos in an easy laundry bag. 15
33. Place a magnet on your hammer's base for nail retrieval. 15
34. Nail polish the tops of your keys to distinguish them. 16

35. Remove "stripped" screws from wood with a rubber band. 16
36. Place socks on your Swiffer Dusters. 16
37. Nail an old rake high on your wall, upside down, for a wineglass holder. 17
38. Create a cutting board over your trashcan. 17
39. Slice up an old plastic hanger to clip up your chips. 18
40. Store knives in many bamboo skewers. 18
41. Place plastic bags in your empty Lysol wipes container. 18
42. Create a dustpan from a milk jug. 18
43. Create plastic bag closers with the top of a regular bottle of water. 19
44. Use an old window shutter to hang utensils and kitchen cloths. 19
45. Use old vintage trophies for utensil storage. 20
46. Utilize brown paper for a long grocery list that's always changing. 20
47. Position dividers in your cabinets utilizing tension curtain rods. 20
48. Position a towel rack on the inside of a cabinet to store lids. 21
49. Use old 2-liter bottles for grain, pasta, and cereal containers. 21
50. Store yarn in old coffee cans. 21
51. Place a tension rod beneath your sink to hang your spray bottles. 22
52. Place a magnetic rack on your kitchen wall to keep knives. 22
53. Place plastic wrap or aluminum foil in a magazine rack. 22
54. Place magnetic spices on your refrigerator. 23
55. Label large bins with "Sugar" or "Flour" and then stack them in your cabinet or cupboard. 23
56. Place your boots on old hangers in your closet. 23
57. Label your hangers for similar-looking clothes. 24
58. Position your eyeglasses and sunglasses on a wooden hanger. 24
59. Position a ribbon on the wall for sunglass or eyeglass storage. 24
60. Use shower curtain hooks to hang your handbags. 25
61. Place Command hooks in your closet to hang necklaces and bracelets. 25
62. Place pool noodles in your boots to keep them upright. 25
63. Place the sheets that match your pillowcases inside the pillowcases. 26
64. Attach a magnified circle to your bathroom cupboard on which to keep your tweezers. 26
65. Create an entire magnetic rack in your bathroom. 26
66. Store bracelets and hair ties on glass bottles. 27
67. Place a shelf over your bathroom door for the things you hardly use. 27
68. Attach baskets to rails on your bathroom wall for enhanced bathroom organization. 27
69. Create a magnetic makeup board with magnetized makeup gear. 28
70. Hang a ladder from your ceiling to hang your wet clothes. 28
71. Store your children's balls with bungee cords. 28
72. Hang your sports gear on a pegboard. 29
73. Create a Mason jar organizer for your screws. 29
74. Look to a clean dustpan for this essential household hack. 29
75. Cover up wooden dings in your furniture with this natural hack. 30
76. Hold your place in a roll of tape with a bread tab. 30

77. Hold a nail with a clothespin. 30
78. Wrap a rubber band around a paint can vertically. 31
79. Use toilet paper rolls to keep wrapping paper under wraps. 31

Chapter 2: DIY Crafts and Parenting Hacks 33

1. Give your children their own personalized, designated cup with attached magnets. 34
2. Place oilcloth over your kids' outdoor picnic table. 34
3. Put Capri Suns in the freezer. 34
4. Choose a sticker to cut in half, placing one half in one shoe, and another half in the other shoe. ...35
5. Use clean restaurant sauce containers for your pacifiers. 35
6. Create this mix to remove stubborn baby food stains from a onesie. 35
7. Fill water balloons with a used soap dispenser. 36
8. Write a message on your child's arm and seal it with a liquid bandage. 36
9. Place a visible sign where kids should cut the toilet paper to reduce waste. 36
10. Rubber band for pencil gripping. 37
11. Place an essential oil on kids' cuts. 37
12. Create faux tap dancing shoes for an excited child. 37
13. Place a "safe" sticker on your car for errands. 37
14. Handle sparklers with a red plastic cup. 38
15. Inflate an outdoor pool inside for a safe area to play. 38
16. Add 2 tbsp. of fabric softener and water to a spray bottle for hairspray for a doll. 38
17. Place glue gun glue in the holes of bath toys. 39
18. Bring shower caddies from the dollar store for Happy Meals and eating in the car. 39
19. Place a crib sheet over a playpen when your baby is outside. 39
20. Utilize an egg carton for greater card game organization. 39
21. Create no-slick shoes with a glue gun. 40
22. Separate your children's different clothing with the "dot" method. 40
23. Create a to-do creativity wallet for your kids at restaurants. 40
24. When you make frozen pops, add some Jell-O so they don't melt. 41
25. Always take a small baby bath to your beach. 41
26. Utilize a super-cheap camera bag for a diaper bag. 41
27. Place a padlock in the hole of your electric plugs. 41
28. Place a puppy pad beneath your child's fitted sheet. 42
29. Place your baby or toddler in a laundry basket in the bathtub so they don't lose their toys. 42
30. Always ask the baby his or her name—whether or not the baby can talk yet. 42
31. Keep your tossed-out cell phones and allow your children to play with them. 43
32. Strengthen your child's upper body with the monkey bars: read on. 43
33. Also add sprinkles. 43
34. Create a fake hammock with a large blanket and a table. 43
35. Always trace your child's feet for solo shoe shopping. 44
36. Tie up a tank top with a barrette. 44
37. Place vapor rub on your children's feet to stop coughing. 44

38. Create a faux-monster spray to spray in your scared child's room. 45
39. Place a single wad of Kleenex beneath your child's two last fingers for proper pencil holding. 45
40. Place a pool noodle on a door for a doorstopper. 45
41. Place a maxi pad in a potty-training kid's diaper during the nighttime. 46
42. Glitz up your money to make it look like it's from the tooth fairy. 46
43. Place a stability ball beneath your children when they're doing homework. 46
44. Place formula or milk in an ice cube tray, and freeze a pacifier on top. 47
45. Give a baby medicine with this one cool hack. 47
46. Create a faux hair tie with a zip tie. 47
47. Create a coloring travel kit with an old DVD case. 47
48. Bring a shower caddy on a long road trip. 48
49. Allow your kids to eat messy snacks while they're in the bathtub. 48
50. Create DIY sock grips so your kids don't go flying on hardwood floors. 48
51. Color scuffed shoes with crayon. 49
52. Create "bed rails" in the hotel. 49
53. Allow your very young children to play with play dough—while it's wrapped up. 49
54. Place a crazy straw in a cup upside down. 49
55. Slice an apple—and then put it back together. 50
56. Use a pizza cutter for easy small food cutting! 50
57. If your child hates the shirt she or he is wearing— 50
58. Remove permanent marker marks on wood with white toothpaste. 51
59. Place a coffee cup lid beneath a frozen pop for easy cleanup. 51
60. Place peas in the pasta shells. 51
61. Place a large, opened cardboard box over your steps. 52
62. "Play video games" with your children with this fun hack. 52
63. Easily remove a splinter DIY. 52
64. Create a fun bracelet with your phone number for your child to wear. 52
65. Spray hot seat belt buckles with a water spray bottle. 53
66. Place pool noodles on every "chain" of your trampoline. 53
67. Remove strawberry stems with a straw. 53
68. Create throwaway plates with your pizza box. 54

Chapter 3: DIY Cleaning and Organizing Hacks 55

1. Remove oil from your stovetop with extra oil. 56
2. Remove microfiber couch stains with rubbing alcohol. 56
3. Shine and cleanse your stovetop with car wax. 56
4. Place vinegar on a sock to clean the blinds. 56
5. Cleanse your burners—without scrubbing. 57
6. Remove water rings with a blow dryer. 57
7. Pull up a carpet stain with an iron. 57
8. Remove oil from the carpet with this awesome hack. 58
9. Wipe down stainless steel with lemon. 58

10. Make a natural tub cleanser. 58
11. Clean up your cast iron pots. 59
12. Steam up a microwave to clean it. 59
13. Vinegar in the coffee pot for cleansing. 59
14. Cream of tartar for stainless steel toaster oven. 60
15. Cleanse your toilet with duct tape and vinegar. 60
16. Clean your windowsills with vinegar and Q-tips. 60
17. Cleanse your computer keyboard with a toothbrush. 61
18. Utilize the top of a ketchup bottle to make "suction" on your vacuum. 61
19. Look to white chalk for greasy stains. 61
20. Don't scrub your shower heads: use this DIY hack. 62
21. Clean up your wall's baseboards with dryer sheets. 62
22. Remove unwanted clothes with this awesome hack. 62
23. Strip off unwanted pot and pan stains with apple peels. 63
24. Clip your car freshener to your central AC unit. 63
25. Mix together baking soda and bleach to cleanse your house of grout mold. 63
26. Create homemade Febreze with this awesome recipe. 64
27. Utilize a lime and some baking soda to clean your sink. 64
28. Always put a cheap kind of soap in your pretty "foam" soap dispensers. 64
29. Remove sticker residue from your jars and cans with this hack. 65
30. Remove clothing grease stains with a bit of dish detergent. 65
31. Mix together hydrogen peroxide and flour to de-stain your granite countertops. 65
32. Add plastic toy to the dishwasher for super-easy cleanup. 66
33. Create homemade clothing wrinkle fighter. 66
34. Fall away from paper towels and save money with this super-easy hack. 66
35. Create "new" soap out of old slivers. 67
36. Create your own laundry soap at home. 67
37. Utilize olive oil to clean your makeup brushes. 68
38. Shine up your brass with a vinegar and flour mix. 68
39. Spray baking soda and water mixture in your oven. 68
40. Make your carpet fresh: instantly. 69
41. Make your own window cleaner. 69
42. Bring shine back to your stainless steel. 69
43. Hand wash your Swiffer duster. 70
44. Clean your dishwasher with this super hack. 70
45. Clean windows and stainless steel with coffee filters. 70
46. Place small, easily lost items in a laundry bag and wash them in the dishwasher. 71
47. Keep silica gel packs. 71
48. Drip a few essential oil drops on your toilet paper roll. 71
49. Place old newspaper at the bottom of your garbage bag. 72
50. Clean up your blender with this essential hack. 72
51. Get fabric "balls" off your clothes and freshen your look with this hack. 72

Chapter 4: DIY Beauty Hacks ... 73

1. Get your lipstick off your teeth. ... 74
2. Utilize white eye shadow to make your eyes pop. ... 74
3. Look to mascara for eyeliner. ... 74
4. Having trouble applying concealer beneath your eyes? Try this unique hack. ... 75
5. Make your regular eyeliner "liquid" in 15 seconds! ... 75
6. Create a beautiful DIY manicure. ... 75
7. Apply baby powder to your lashes for stunning lash power. ... 76
8. Make an X in the center of your top lip to apply proper lip liner. ... 76
9. Remove split ends. ... 76
10. Quickly style your hair with a topknot. ... 76
11. Create your own DIY dry shampoo. ... 77
12. Get perfect winged eyeliner. ... 77
13. Fix up your French manicure with a rubber band. ... 77
14. Place a business card above your lashes for perfect eyelash mascara application. ... 78
15. Create awesome nail art with a Band-Aid. ... 78
16. Always check your makeup in the natural light of your car. ... 78
17. Always have one makeup brush for applying and one for blending. ... 79
18. Remove glitter nail polish with Elmer's Glue. ... 79
19. Create a manicure with Elmer's Glue, as well. ... 79
20. Utilize eye shadow on your lips for the perfect, full lip color. ... 79
21. Flat iron your braids for awesome waves. ... 80
22. Bring light into the dark corners of your eyes. ... 80
23. Apply perfume like a pro. ... 80
24. Make your nail polish set more quickly. ... 81
25. Put mouthwash on your bruises. ... 81
26. DIY bronzer with at-home ingredients. ... 81
27. Remove makeup from your shirt collars with this essential hack. ... 81
28. Make your pimples slightly less visible with Visine. ... 82
29. DIY your own lip stain. ... 82
30. Create a leave-in conditioner. ... 82
31. Create a "long" ponytail with short hair. ... 83
32. Use hand cream to smooth frizzing hair. ... 83
33. Run a dryer sheet through staticky hair. ... 83
34. Remove all makeup with coconut oil. ... 83
35. Make a baking soda at-home mask to remove blackheads. ... 84
36. Treat your cuticles with lip gloss. ... 84
37. Use conditioner for shaving cream. ... 84
38. Place deodorant on the inside of your thighs to keep from chafing. ... 84
39. Skip over the eyeliner step with this awesome beauty hack. ... 85
40. Avoid people noticing your chipping manicure with this unique hack. ... 85
41. Utilize lipstick for blush when you're on-the-go. ... 85

42. Combine highlighter with your body lotion. 86
43. Look to clear mascara to seal your black lashes. 86
44. Use a credit card to maximize your "cat eye" look. 86
45. Look to peppermint oil to boost your lip look. 86
46. Curl your eyelashes and apply your eyeliner at the same time. 87
47. Utilize white eyeliner to hide a hangover. 87
48. Lighten foundation with white moisturizer. 87
49. Warm up your mascara before applying it with this unique hack. 88
50. Place Vaseline on your wrists or neck before you apply perfume. 88
51. Spread a bit of white makeup pencil to the center of your lip to bring layered shine. 88
52. Focus on only one element of your face when you're limited on time. 89
53. Add contact solution to your clumpy mascara. 89
54. Keep a few face wipes by your bed if you don't want to wash your face every night. 89
55. Sleep with two pillows—not one—to reduce puffy eyes. 90
56. Make your lipstick "matte" without buying matte lipstick. 90
57. Heal your feet while you sleep. 90
58. Make your smile brighter by brushing with baking soda. 90
59. Halt runs in your tights with hairspray. 91
60. Get rid of stretch marks with baby oil. 91
61. Make your hair look full with a bit of eye shadow. 91
62. Eliminate your up-do flyaways with this awesome hack. 91
63. Keep your bobby pins in place with hairspray. 92
64. T-shirts are better at drying your hair than towels. 92
65. Wash your roots in the sink. 92

Chapter 5: Fitness and Exercise Hacks 93

1. Listen to your favorite podcast ONLY when you exercise. 94
2. Try the above with your favorite audio book. 94
3. Buy good-looking workout clothes. 94
4. Download an app like jog.fm. 94
5. Create an exercise schedule and make sure to stick to it. 95
6. Run one minute per day and add an additional minute every day. 95
7. Run with a partner and talk the whole time. 95
8. Create an "exercise" game during your favorite television show. 95
9. Create an exercise playlist with the exact amount of exercise time you want. 96
10. Keep some gym clothes and shoes with you at all times. 96
11. Sleep in your exercise clothes for early-morning workouts. 96
12. Place frozen fruit in your regular water bottle. 97
13. Wrap plastic wrap around your touchscreen phone if it's about to rain on your run. 97
14. Find a mid-television exercise you could do. 97
15. Cycle on the exercise bike and play video games on your television. 98
16. Always make yourself "work" for your snacks. 98

17. Give yourself two dollars every time you exercise rather than joining a gym. 98
18. Make your own DIY weights at home. 99
19. Look to purchase a pedometer to enhance your step numbers. 99
20. Watch personal trainers at the gym instead of hiring your own. 99
21. Look for steps. 100
22. Schedule text reminders to yourself to tell yourself to exercise. 100
23. Always go for a walk to clear your mind and de-stress yourself. 100
24. Always get some "fun" exercise on vacation. 100
25. Try cleaning the house. 101
26. If you live in a big city, sell your car. 101
27. Adopt a dog. 101
28. Ask for a standing desk at work. 102
29. Go out dancing instead of to a pub. 102
30. Go to the gym when people are "away." 102
31. wear while you're exercising. (Maybe not in public.) 103
32. Always write down all of the food you eat. 103
33. Skip milk and sugar and try cinnamon. 103
34. Always use a small plate rather than a dinner plate. 103
35. Always use fresh vegetables rather than canned vegetables. 104
36. Never watch television and eat at the same time. 104

Chapter 6: DIY Tips to Make Your Life Easier 105

1. Heat up your microwavable leftovers with more efficiency. 106
2. Stack all your dresser clothes in a vertical fashion. 106
3. Chew gum while you're slicing onions. 106
4. Create a stand for your iPhone with an old cassette case. 106
5. When you're almost finished eating your jar of Nutella with a spoon, look to this delicious hack. 107
6. Make sure you drink enough water with this hack. 107
7. Iron your collar with your hair straightener. 107
8. Bring your bagel to work in a container you already have. 108
9. Create pancake mix ahead of time and pour it into a ketchup bottle. 108
10. Sick of having friends borrow things and never return them? 108
11. Serve condiments in a muffin tin at large outdoor parties. 108
12. Slice cakes and cheeses perfectly with dental floss. 109
13. Tab your straw to keep it in place. 109
14. Bake tortillas in upside-down muffin pans. 109
15. Always position a square of cardboard in your plastic bags. 110
16. Light candles with a stick of spaghetti. 110
17. Freeze your sponges to make ice packs. 110
18. Use bread tabs to label your cords. 110
19. Make "bacon" pancakes. 111
20. Use a nice pool noodle to make your beer cooler float. 111

21. Keep your stuff safe at the beach with this all-too-clever hack. 111
22. Find lost, tiny items by placing an old stocking over your vacuum cleaner tube. 112
23. Keep your pot from boiling over with this unique hack. 112
24. Hold cookbooks up high with a pants hanger. 112
25. Make your bottles ice-cold instantly. 113
26. Make hanging pictures easy today! 113
27. Create your own ice packs at home! 113
28. Dry your wet shoes in the dryer with this unique hack. 113
29. Create a watering can from an old milk carton. 114

Chapter 7: DIY Recipes and Cooking Hacks 115

1. Cut corn off the cob with this super-easy hack. 116
2. Core iceberg lettuce instantly. 116
3. Cook pasta in about one minute. 116
4. Pit an avocado with a knife. 116
5. Create neat avocado cubes while the avocado is in the skin. 117
6. Eat a kiwi straight from the skin. 117
7. Alternately, peel the kiwi with the spoon from the inside out. 117
8. Keep your cutting board still while you're cutting on it. 117
9. Stop allowing your butter to "thaw" before cutting it with this baking trick. 118
10. Slice all your cherry tomatoes or grapes all at once. 118
11. Add baking soda to caramelize your onions FAST. 118
12. De-husk your corn FAST. 118
13. Spread nonstick spray over your cheese grater for easy grating. 119
14. Get ALL the juice from lemons and limes. 119
15. Peel a head of garlic instantly. 119
16. Make "French fries" with an apple slicer. 119
17. Peel your potatoes in an instant. 120
18. Slice meat easily with this DIY hack. 120
19. Take out cherry pits in a flash. 120
20. Make "whipped" cream easily. 120
21. Take the peels off a dozen boiled eggs at once. 121
22. Remove scattered eggshells from eggs easily. 121
23. Make waffle iron hash browns. 121
24. Open a candy kiss the right way. 121
25. Make instant cheese bread. 122
26. Make an omelet on a panini maker. 122
27. Make pancake pops with spare "sucker" straws. 122
28. Create "milk and cookie" ice cubes or the perfect chocolate drink. 123
29. Make your salads easily inside of a jar. 123
30. Know what to do with asparagus. 123
31. Make pancakes with cookie cutters. 123

- 32. Make fun eggs the same exact way. ... 124
- 33. Eat a cupcake the right way. ... 124
- 34. Boil oatmeal water in your Keurig. ... 124
- 35. Make an "egg" burger. ... 125
- 36. Seal your bags with your own CO_2 and keep your food fresh. ... 125
- 37. Place your ice cream cartons inside of zip-lock bags. ... 125

Conclusion: ... 127

Introduction

365 Days of DIY brings you awesome do-it-yourself household hacks, parenting hacks, cleaning hacks, beauty hacks, fitness hacks, essential life hacks, and cooking hacks. Do you feel that your life has become mundane, slow, and all-too-difficult? If you want to maximize your lifestyle, become the most creative element of your own life, and fuel yourself with ready discipline to yield essential vibrancy through gift-giving, cleaning, and weight loss endeavors, you NEED this book. Seriously.

This entire year's worth of DIY hacks will make your life infinitely easier. All the things currently surrounding you—from your ceiling fans to your socks—you can utilize to make a sort of "magic" in your personal environment.

Best of all: you can create DIY gifts with an end "gift" at the back of this book. 45 DIY Christmas Gifts offers excellent ideas for homemade skin care scrubs, recipes, beauty supplies, play dough—and so much more. You get 365 ideas to maximize your entire year. On top of that, you get 45 DIY Christmas gift ideas to allow you to save money AND give awesome homemade gifts at the end of the year. Wow. You really can maximize every element of your day.

Become your most creative version of yourself. Become a person brimming with beauty, with engagement. You are the master of your domain. You are the master of DIY. You don't have to spend thousands of dollars every year to join a gym, to clean your house, to become the best kind of parent, or to deliver the best Christmas gifts ever. All you need is this book, a bit of supplies, and some determination. Your life is brimming with possibility. Grab it!

Enjoy the following DIY hacks to maximize your life and create stunning beauty!

Chapter 1: DIY Household Hacks and DIY Projects

Think of your house: it's hard to manage, isn't it? If only you had a few household hacks to help you really take charge of your house with organization and style. Follow these around-the-house hacks in order to brighten your home, make it easy to manage, and keep it lively and clean!

1.
Position old doorknobs in your bathroom to hang clothes and towels.

So often, your bathroom doesn't have enough hanging space—and those ratty towels end up everywhere: from over your door to crumpled on the floor. Utilize this household hack to better your bathroom sensibilities today.

A. First, gather up any old doorknobs you have lying around your house. Make sure they still have their "backing" to them—the metal piece that used to be positioned on your door. Note that you can probably find these at local antique stores, as well.

B. P aint the doorknobs any color you please to match your bathroom.

C. Position the old doorknobs across your bathroom wall and screw or nail them into the wall securely.

D. Hang your towels and clothes on the doorknobs for a cute DIY fix.

2.
Create a bracelet holder on an older paper towel holder.

So often, your bracelets end up crumpled on the floor, tangled in an old drawer, or lost to the winds! Find the perfect bracelet to match your outfit right now when you position your bracelets on an old paper towel holder, perfect to catch your eye before you exit your home.

A. Find an old paper towel holder—without a roll on it.

B. Paint it whatever color you like so that it matches your bedroom. Position the painted paper towel holder in your room, perhaps on your bureau.

C. Position your bracelets on the paper towel holder to organize them neatly so that they're laid out in front of you, easy for you to see.

3.
Hide your ugly thermostat behind a hinged painting.

Your thermostat is a horrid, blinking appliance that can interrupt the beauty of any room. Utilize this clever hack to hide your thermostat behind your favorite canvas.

    A. Choose a large, pretty painting or photo on canvas.

    B. Place two flat hinges on the back of the canvas and then mount them to the wall in an appropriate place. Note that you can pick up these hinges at your local hardware store.

    C. Simply open and close the photo or painting canvas whenever you want to alter the thermostat, and don't look at the ugly thing anymore if you don't want to!

4.
Paint your walls with polka dots with an old laundry basket.

Have you tried to paint polka dots, only to become disappointed when your polka dots look a little lopsided? Utilize this clever hack to paint polka dots in any room of your house, on any cabinet, and on any piece of clothing!

    A. Tape an old laundry basket with circular holes to your wall with duct tape.

    B. Paint the insides of the circles with your paint color of choice. Let paint dry.

    C. Move the laundry basket, making sure not to disturb the paint, and continue down the line.

5.
Create beautiful shelves with your old dresser drawers.

When you want to get rid of your old dresser, don't toss away the old shelves. Instead, dress them up for remarkable, illuminating shelves you can tack onto your wall, anywhere you want!

    A. Remove your old dresser drawer, complete with the back.

    B. Paint the dresser drawer your color of choice.

    C. Nail the back of the drawer to your wall in a place of choice, and place your favorite items:

flowers, bracelets, necklaces—anything you want!—in the drawer. Enjoy!

6.
Use a wine rack for a kitchen towel holder.

Again, with the towels! But seriously: your lifestyle is amok with too many towels. Arrange them beautifully in your kitchen by hanging up an old-fashioned wine rack, and then spinning each of the towels into the wine rack. You don't even have to alter anything about the wine rack, if you don't want!

7.
Hang your ironing board on two coat hangers.

Coat hangers are super-easy to find at your local hardware store, and they become essential elements of your home when you want to hang your loathsome ironing board. Remember that thing? The ironing board that's currently taking up too much space in your closet—the very thing that always falls on your head when you open the door? Hang it on some coat hangers.

A. Measure the length of your ironing board's "feet."

B. Position two coat hangers this distance from each other on the wall in your closet. Screw them in with their included directions. Make sure to make them high enough on the wall to allow your ironing board to hang.

C. Hang the coat hanger, and retrieve it any time you need without the usual hassle.

8.
Use a shoe organizer to organize your snacks in the pantry!

Your pantry is a constant mess. Fruit snacks are falling on the flour; power bars are chucked to the back end. Where are the crazy straws? Where should you keep the seasoning packets? Gosh, life is hard. But not so with this awesome hack.

A. Hang a plastic shoe organizer on the door of your pantry.

B. Position your favorite snacks in their homes in the shoe organizer.

C. If you please, you can organize each of the plastic pockets by taping labels on them.

9.
Use an old '90s CD tower for your bathroom organization.

All the stuff you have in your bathroom: your contact solution, your toothpaste, your pills, and your unmentionables, can come together easily with this awesome home hack. Everyone who lived through the explosion of CDs has an old CD tower. During this digital age, it's time to put that thing to good use.

A. Clean and paint your old CD tower however you please.

B. Place the CD tower with the compartments facing up, in the area around your sink, below your mirror.

C. Nail the CD tower into place, making sure it's completely level using a level.

D. Place your favorite bathroom supplies in the CD tower, and enjoy your new organization!

10.
Pour your cleaning solution or laundry detergent into a drink dispenser.

Okay: so. That ugly Tide bottle currently living in your house has to go. Pour the stuff into a clear drink dispenser to easily retrieve it when you do laundry. You won't have to utilize anything so bright and ugly as a Tide container in your laundry room. Instead, you can live a refined life!

11.
Place magazine racks in your pantry to store your cans.

Cans and cans and cans. They're filling your pantry space, and they're falling all over the place when you open the pantry door. Sigh.

Never fear. Simply place an old magazine rack in your pantry and place the cans horizontally in the thing in a great stack. This way, you can see all the cans well, and you know they're all in the same spot! Awesome.

12.
Keep a bit of extra room paint in a small baby food jar, for easy touch-ups.

Every time you paint a room, you surely think you've gotten every single spot. But then: a week, a month, or even a year later, you might notice something—a small speck of the old color—that you didn't notice before. When you keep a bit of the color in a baby food jar, you can quickly touch up the paint without going back to the store and trying to find the same paint. (Because your garage has surely already eaten your old can of the paint by then, anyway.)

13.
Better spare key hiding than ever before.

We all know the importance of keeping your spare key somewhere safe. This year, instead of keeping it under the mat, check out this awesome home hack.

- A. Place your spare key in a medicine bottle.
- B. Glue a small pinecone to the end of the medicine bottle.
- C. Bury the medicine bottle in the yard with the pinecone above ground.

14.
Place another shower curtain rod in your shower for better storage opportunities.

Your shower is a mess, usually. After all: all those loofas and washcloths can really escalate the messiness, making you feel dirty even when you exit the shower. If you hang another rod on the other side of your shower, across from the curtain, you can place hooks on it that can hold extra things like loofas and washcloths. You can even hang special soaps or a waterproof radio!

15.
Use dry erase marker on your bathroom mirror for helpful hints and reminders.

When you utilize dry erase marker on things other than white boards, the magic really escalates in your life. Make yourself a list in your favorite colors of dry erase marker the evening before you need to remember something, and when you're brushing your teeth the next day, your day's events will unfold before your eyes. Simply wipe them clean with soap, water, or Clorox wipes, and continue your dry erase marker journey!

16.
Place a phone book in the back of deep storage spaces to keep track of everything.

This is maybe a little hard to follow, but bear with me. When you place a phone book horizontally and deep in the back of your storage space and then line up books or movies on the phone book, you can keep track of everything you have. You can see the tops of your movies in the back, even when you line your movies up in front of the phone book. See? Two layers—easily created with that phone book you thought you'd never use again.

17.
Screw foam noodles into the walls of your garage.

How often have you opened up your car door and slammed it into your garage wall? Your door is ruined; your wall is ruined. Nothing will be good again! However: when you attach foam noodles into your wall, your doors can bounce back at you, unharmed.

    A. Slice a long foam noodle in half, vertically, so that you create a flat edge.

365 Days of DIY

B. Screw or nail the foam noodle into the wall, making sure that the noodle is in the exact area that your door usually hits. (You'll probably see the marks on the wall.)

18.
Create a eucalyptus fragrance explosion in your shower.

Make your shower experience even more magical with some stress-relieving eucalyptus. You can find some eucalyptus leaves at your local garden store. Simply attach the foliage to your showerhead with rubber bands or the twisty ties you get from your bread bags. Allow the magic to take hold the next time you run the hot water. Your shower will explode with wonderful fragrance. Furthermore, eucalyptus has been shown to be anti-stress and super-relieving.

19.
Store cords on plastic hangers.

The things we accumulate in life: plastic hangers and old cords—from our televisions, our computers, our old recorders, everything. Find this way to store your cords well without tangling them.

- A. Remove the "hanger" part of the clothes hanger, but keep the body—where the clothes normally go.
- B. Wrap your cords around the "body" part, and store the cords all together, unafraid that they'll wrap up together and become tangled.

20.
Hide your Internet router with fake books.

How funny is this? So often, we're bogged down by how ugly our Internet routers are. However, if you utilize this super-literary hack, you can put charm and beauty into your living room once more!

- A. Measure your router with regards to a few hardcover second-hand books you don't mind destroying. Note that the router has to fit in between the two outside book covers.

B. Remove the pages from all of the books with an X-acto knife. You can do this with one fell swoop. You need to end up with only the hard covers.

C. Next, decide which books you want on the end of your "hider." Remove keep the back end of one of the book covers and keep the front end of one of the book covers, and remove all other covers to create an empty space behind the "titles."

D. Glue the covers together, making them look like they are books lined up on a shelf. Place the router behind the book covers, hidden by the two sides of one end of one book and one end of the far book. Tape or glue the router into place back there, and keep the router wherever you usually do—with the remarkable "hack" of making it look quite literary.

21.
Remove the indentations from your carpet with ice cubes.

Those indentations in your carpet from furniture can be removed easily with ice cubes! Simply position ice cubes over the indentation, about two inches apart from each other, and wait for five minutes. The indentations should rise.

22.
Keep your door open with a rubber band.

When you're going in and out of your door repeatedly, you probably want to keep your door open. But when it automatically closes on you, life can get a bit tricky! Simply keep the door open by wrapping a rubber band around one of the handles, spinning it around over the "latch," and then positioning it over the other door handle. This way, the "latch" will stay inside of the door, allowing the door to stay open as you come in and out!

23.
Organize your plastic bags with a Kleenex box.

Tissue boxes go empty quickly—especially during flu season. Keep some of your favorite designs and stock them with plastic bags. This way, you can organize your plastic bags well, you can keep the pretty box, and you can find plastic bags whenever you need to!

24.
Plop a ball of aluminum foil into your dryer for a better dryer sheet!

If you use a dryer sheet every time you dry your clothes, those things really add up! Instead, simply form a few balls from aluminum foil and toss them into your dryer. They're awesome and reusable. Furthermore, they completely take the static out of your clothes.

25.
Remove pet hair from your carpet with a window squeegee.

Hello, remarkable world! Pet hair and dander are very real things, making your living room a few shades of dismal. However, when you utilize a window squeegee and go over your carpet easily, just skimming the top like you would a window, you can remove all the pet hair. Make sure to continually remove the pet hair from the edge of the squeegee in order to keep it picking up the hair efficiently. Enjoy your new, hairless living room!

26.
Position your storage bag and garbage bag cardboard containers in your pantry with thumbtacks.

Your cardboard boxes with garbage bags and storage bags can get lost in the mess of your pantry, absolutely. However, when you position your cardboard containers in your pantry in the precise places you know to look for them, you can tack them to the wall for an easy grab. Simply use a thumbtack and drive it through the top of the cardboard container to allow it to hang down.

27.
Position Christmas lights in your closet for better lighting.

How often are you unable to find things in your closet, just because you don't get proper lighting back there? You want to see your clothes, your shoes, and your accessories well—and you want them to look good in there, don't you? Simply line the inside doorway of your closet with Christmas lights! I used white, but you can really use whatever light colors you want.

28.
Position your shower hooks on your closet rod to make clothes accessible.

Jeans can be a serious hassle to hang. However, when you hook them up to old shower hooks—the very hooks you used to utilize in order to hang a shower curtain, for example—you can see all the old jeans you used to have and wear them again! Plus, the jeans look really, really good hanging this way.

    A. Remove your shower curtain from the hooks.

    B. Position the hooks on the closet rod, and hang the jeans below.

29.
Position a magnetic strip of tape beneath your food or storage cabinets to place metal-topped spices beneath.

Your cooking spices are the best part of your kitchen. They're essential for every element of your cooking lifestyle. Therefore, you need to know where they are!

- A. Measure the length of the area you wish to be magnetic. Make sure you understand the width or radius of the spice caps you will be using, as well. This all goes into play when you position your magnetic strip beneath your cabinets.

- B. Pick up a magnetic tape roll at your local hardware store.

- C. Cut the magnetic tape to the appropriate length and width, and position it beneath your cabinet. Note that it's already sticky.

- D. Afterwards, simply tap the metal heads of your spices to this magnetic strip, and reap the rewards of an organized kitchen.

30.
Place a letter organizer in your closet to organize flat shoes.

Your shoes, especially those flip flops and flats, find their way around your house like nothing else you own. Stick your old letter organizers in your closet and place your flip flops and flats in each section, together. This way: you'll always know where to find them and where to put them. They fit snugly, and they're out-of-sight. (They are, after all, your everyday shoes—nothing you want to display.)

31.
Place a Command hook on the other side of your baby's high chair for bib-hanging.

How often do you search for you baby's bib in the moments before your baby feasts? Pretty much all the time, am I right? Well, if you place an easy Command hook on the other side of your baby's high chair, you'll have an easy place to hang your baby's clean bibs. This way, you can simply reach around, grab a baby bib, and attach the bib to your baby's neck mid munch.

32.
Disinfect Legos in an easy laundry bag.

When your children's Legos end up sticky, gross, and riddled with bacteria, you have to take immediate action. Legos are super-prone to disease. Therefore, the next time your children have a play date—or your children have a cold—it's best to toss the Legos into the washing machine.

A. Place the Legos in a laundry bag.

B. Start your washing machine and administer your normal amount of detergent.

C. Wait until the machine is full of soapy water before tossing the Lego-filled bag into the mess.

D. Close the machine and let it run a full cycle.

E. Allow the bag to drip-dry before using the Legos again.

33.
Place a magnet on your hammer's base for nail retrieval.

When you're doing a bit of DIY at home, you probably have to interact with nails and hammers a good deal. How often, when you do this, do you plop your nails in your mouth, ready whenever you need them? I thought so.

Now, you can glue a magnet to the base of your normal hammer. When you hammer away, you can have the nails already attached to the hammer, ready for immediate retrieval. This way, your hammering is no longer a safety hazard to yourself. You will be under no danger of swallowing those suckers. Phew!

34.
Nail polish the tops of your keys to distinguish them.

Count how many keys you currently have on your key chain. A lot, right? And how often do you reach for one key only to have to hunt for another key—and another? When you differentiate the keys, you can keep your life a little more organized, every single day.

Simply paint the tops of each of your keys with a different nail polish color. Allow them to dry, and then position them back on your keychain. Try to match up colors with different things that match: blue for dead BOLT, green for outdoor shed, etc.

35.
Remove "stripped" screws from wood with a rubber band.

Struggling with removing a stripped screw? Every time you place your screwdriver into the screw, it simply rolls and rolls around, never allowing you to remove the stubborn thing from the wood. Never fear! If you simply place a rubber band immediately over the indent in the screw and then place the screwdriver on top of the rubber band, you can bring that thing up. Use adequate pressure, and make sure the rubber band stays in place beneath the screwdriver. Enjoy this awesome hack!

36.
Place socks on your Swiffer Dusters.

Old socks come in handy when you don't want to keep buying those expensive Swiffer Duster covers. Simply wrap old chenille socks over the Swiffer head, and clean away. When you're done, toss the socks in the washing machine and reuse as many times as you like! Enjoy!

37.
Nail an old rake high on your wall, upside down, for a wineglass holder.

Nothing screams rustic kitchen like a rake hanging upside down on the wall. Add some hanging wineglasses to its tongs and create the most beautiful wine station in the world: where refined taste meets country.

A. Remove the metal from the wooden handle of a large rake.

B. Wrap picture wire around the new metal "handle," and hang the rake over a hook.

C. Hang wineglasses from the tongs, and voila!

38.
Create a cutting board over your trashcan.

When you're slicing and dicing your meats, vegetables, and fruits, it's always a hassle to carry all the waste from the cutting board all the way to your trashcan. Usually, you can't even get everything in one trip!

Instead of messing with that, create a cutting board in one of your drawers, and allow it to pull out over a trashcan for ready cleaning.

A. Pick a drawer that is convenient to pull out over a trashcan.

B. Place a flat cutting board—that can be easily taken out and put back in—in the drawer. Create a hole in both the drawer and the cutting board with a five-inch radius.

C. Cut the hole in both the drawer and the cutting board utilizing a jigsaw. Make sure to properly sand the exterior of both the drawer and the cutting board moving forward to eliminate risk of splinters.

D. Place the cutting board in your drawer, pull the drawer out, cut your items, and toss the items through the hole into the trashcan below. Enjoy!

39.
Slice up an old plastic hanger to clip up your chips.

You know those plastic hangers with the "clips" on either end? They come with nearly every item of clothing you purchase from regular retail stores, and you probably have a few lying around your house. Using an X-acto knife or another sharp object, such as craft scissors, cut through the plastic hanger to release just the clips from their prison on the hanger. Utilize the clips to close chip bags and keep your food items from becoming stale.

40.
Store knives in many bamboo skewers.

If you don't want to purchase a knife holder, it's essential that you look to this DIY technique to keep yourself safe—and beautify your kitchen. Simply bring together about a hundred bamboo skewers and place them tightly in a can or glass. Position the knives in the bamboo skewers so that they can't move around but they can be easily removed.

41.
Place plastic bags in your empty Lysol wipes container.

Plastic bags seem to accumulate, don't they? And yet: we always need them for mundane tasks, like dog walking and house cleaning. After you've finished with your recent Lysol wipes container (or another similar container), simply fill that container with old plastic bags. This way, you can just grab and go whenever you please!

42.
Create a dustpan from a milk jug.

This one is pretty hilarious, actually. Dustpans can be pretty pricey, and yet you probably already have the DIY utensils to create your own right now.

A. Create a triangle with a marker on your milk carton by starting at the indent, going "horizontally" to the right across to where the indent stops, heading southwest to the point—directly beneath the handle and at the very bottom of the milk carton.

B. Then, meet up with the initial marker mark to make a triangle.

C. Cut along this point, and then remove the handle of the milk carton at the very top, by the milk carton top. You've created a perfect dustpan, complete with a handle!

43.
Create plastic bag closers with the top of a regular bottle of water.

So often, my various plastic-bag-stored items become stale in my cabinet. However, with this latest DIY household trick, I don't need to work too hard to keep my things very well preserved. This DIY technique utilizes just whatever plastic bag you are currently storing something in and the very top of a bottle of water.

A. Use scissors to insert a cut about one inch below the "mouth hole" of the water bottle. Cut all the way around.

B. Next, bring the top of the bag through the top of the water bottle.

C. Close the water bottle with its cap, creating a perfect seal.

44.
Use an old window shutter to hang utensils and kitchen cloths.

Those pretty window shutters you had to take off your house the other day can come in handy in your kitchen with this awesome DIY hack. Simply attach plastic hooks in various places around the pretty window shutter and then hang your various spatulas, cloths, cheese graters, etc., from the window shutter. Nail the window shutter to a nice place in your kitchen and retrieve your utensils anytime you like! Of course, be sure the shutter is clean and if necessary paint it before hanging it.

45.
Use old vintage trophies for utensil storage.

If your husband or wife was once a "baller," as they say, you probably have several trophies around your house. (Furthermore, if you have kids, you'll start accumulating those trophies sometime soon, as well.) Use those trophies in your kitchen! They're perfect for display, and they're just the right size to place different spoons, utensils, whisks—anything!

46.
Utilize brown paper for a long grocery list that's always changing.

Position a large roll of brown paper at the top of your kitchen wall, by the ceiling, on a large rod. Screw a large yardstick into the wall up by the top on the yardstick's two ends, making sure to pull the brown paper through the center of the yard stick. This way, the brown paper sticks to the wall and can be continually ripped to a fine edge. Write your groceries, your reminders—anything on the list, and then rip it off to deliver new brown paper from the top whenever you please! This is a super-fun and essential way to stay organized.

47.
Position dividers in your cabinets utilizing tension curtain rods.

If you want to keep your baking sheets separate in your cabinets but don't have the money to create a whole new organization system, look to tension curtain rods. Simply position them: one in front and one in back, in the cabinet. Create as many dividers between the baking sheets as you like, and then slide the baking sheets in between the different aisles. Enjoy your newly organized kitchen.

48.
Position a towel rack on the inside of a cabinet to store lids.

Pot lids never seem to stack right, do they, leaving you to hunt everywhere for wherever the last one slid off to. With this DIY trick, you can easily position the pot lids in a readily available place.

    A. Attach a towel rack on the inside of a cabinet with the included instructions.

    B. Slide the top of the pots into the towel racks, catching the holder with the towel rod.

49.
Use old 2-liter bottles for grain, pasta, and cereal containers.

When your life is a bumbling mess of cereals, pasta bags, and various containers of oatmeal, things can get out of hand. However, when you utilize old 2-liter bottles for containers, you can see everything out on the counter, beautifully displayed and kept safe from becoming stale. Check out this step-by-step DIY hack.

    A. About a third of the way down on your naked 2-liter bottle, insert your scissors and slice all the way around in a straight circle.

    B. Next, take another 2-liter bottle, and slice similarly about a quarter of the way from the bottom.

    C. Pour your pasta or grains into the larger end of the first 2-liter bottle, and then top the bottle with the bottom of the second bottle. Place all the filled bottles on the counter, and enjoy the view!

50.
Store yarn in old coffee cans.

If you buy coffee cans all the time, why not use those super-useful-sized containers to maximize your organization? You can even paint the outsides of the coffee cans if you want! Simply load each of the cans with yarn, and don't bother keeping the tops. Position the coffee cans horizontally on a shelf so that you can see all of the colors of yarn separately.

51.
Place a tension rod beneath your sink to hang your spray bottles.

The mess beneath your sink doesn't have to be so catastrophic anymore! If you simply place a tension rod horizontally beneath your sink and then hang all your spray bottles on the tension rod, you can create space beneath the hanging spray bottles for even more cleaning supplies. The creation of two levels really maximizes your under-the-sink space.

52.
Place a magnetic rack on your kitchen wall to keep knives.

Despite their scary persona, knives are quite beautiful when they hang all together on the oft-seen magnetic rack in most high-end kitchens. Create your own with an awesome magnetic rack, picked up at your local hardware store. Simply screw the magnetic rack into a wall, and then allow each of the knives to magnetize to the rack. Note that the magnetic rack should be sufficiently pegged to the wall to prevent falling.

53.
Place plastic wrap or aluminum foil in a magazine rack.

Magazine racks are an essential element in organizing things beyond your People and your Entertainment. Place your plastic wraps and your aluminum foils in the magazine rack, vertically, and then place the magazine rack in your cabinet or cupboard. Simply reach in, grab your wrap, and then place the wrap back in the magazine rack whenever you need to. You'll always know where to find it!

54.
Place magnetic spices on your refrigerator.

At the department or craft store, you can surely find magnetic containers. In these magnetic containers, you can place your favorite spices: your nutmegs, your oreganos, your basils, etc. (Make sure to label them!) Then, simply position the spices on your refrigerator for easy access. They're super-pretty, especially if you get clear-topped magnetic containers so that you can see all the awesome accents of the spices! (If you have stainless steel for your fridge, though, magnets likely won't stick to it, and you will need to put a magnetic strip up elsewhere.)

55.
Label large bins with "Sugar" or "Flour" and then stack them in your cabinet or cupboard.

If you are a constant baker, you should look to this awesome DIY technique to always know where your things are, keep your ingredients out of loathsome, ripped packages, and keep everything organized! Simply pour your big-time ingredients into large, clear containers, top them with their sealable tops, and stick them in the cupboard with their labels out toward you.

56.
Place your boots on old hangers in your closet.

Remember those hangers we keep talking about? The old, plastic ones with the clips that you pick up on your retail shopping adventures? Well. If you just clip those clips onto your favorite pairs of long, fashionable boots, you can hang your boots in your closet for easy reaching. Furthermore, those boots look super-fashionable when you open your closet, giving you more reason to look super-good, yourself.

57.
Label your hangers for similar-looking clothes.

How often do you pull out a pair of jeans only to figure out you've pulled out your low-rise rather than your boot-cut? Ugh. It's a disaster, isn't it? If you simply write precisely what items are, what you normally wear those items with, and maybe even some helpful instructions to get yourself ready in the morning, you can hang these tags on the hanger. Position your pants (or whatever) on these hangers to allow your morning self to grab precisely what you're looking for—the first time.

58.
Position your eyeglasses and sunglasses on a wooden hanger.

Wooden hangers—so unlike those clip-on hangers we've been discussing—are essential for your eyeglass storage. If you wear a lot of sunglasses or give yourself a lot of eyeglass options, look to the wooden hanger to hang each of the glasses together safely. This way, they all wind up in the same spot, perfect for your fashion choices.

59.
Position a ribbon on the wall for sunglass or eyeglass storage.

If you would rather have your glasses hanging in the open, try using this DIY ribbon trick. Simply nail both ends of a one-foot long piece of ribbon on the wall. Next, hang each of your sunglasses or eyeglasses from the ribbon. This provides a beautiful way to keep yourself organized.

If you want to keep things interesting, you can even hang a different colored ribbon beneath the first ribbon to create multiple layers.

60.
Use shower curtain hooks to hang your handbags.

Those good old shower curtain hooks come to excellent use when you remove their shower curtain. Position the hooks on your closet's hanging rod, and then hang each of your so-often-lost purses from the hooks. This way, you can see all that you have—and you can remember what you haven't used in a while!

61.
Place Command hooks in your closet to hang necklaces and bracelets.

So often, your necklaces and bracelets become tangled and unorganized. This awesome DIY hack brings organization back to your jewelry. Simply position Command hooks on the door of your closet and hang each of the pieces of jewelry on one of them. This way, you can see everything you have and choose whichever piece you most want to wear—rather than whichever one you just found.

62.
Place pool noodles in your boots to keep them upright.

From pool noodles to boots, so go the seasons, am I right? Measure the height of your boots and slice your pool noodles accordingly. Place the pool noodles upright in your boots to keep them straight, without falling over. Remember: when your boots fall over, they become wrinkled and scattered all over your room. This technique keeps everything centered.

63.
Place the sheets that match your pillowcases inside the pillowcases.

So: you probably have a ton of different pillowcases and sheets floating around your house. Sometimes, it's difficult to find everything when your house seems like a mess of supplies. If you want to keep everything organized, simply place your folded sheets inside the pillowcase they match up with. This way, everything is together. You can keep your naked pillowcases someplace else.

64.
Attach a magnified circle to your bathroom cupboard on which to keep your tweezers.

If you're always looking for your tweezers, you might want to check out this awesome DIY hack. Place a small, magnetized circle on the inside of your cabinet, and always put your tweezers on the magnetized piece. This way: you'll always know where your tweezers are. Pretty cool, no?

65.
Create an entire magnetic rack in your bathroom.

Rather than just keeping your magnetic DIY hacks in tweezers land, create this DIY hack with an entire hardware store-bought magnetic rack. Simply position it on the wall of your bathroom and magnetize to it everything you want to keep track of: your small bathroom scissors, your eyelash curlers, your bobby pins, and everything else.

66.
Store bracelets and hair ties on glass bottles.

Those beautiful glass bottles can have a life post-drink. Position the cleaned glass bottles either in your room or in the bathroom, and line them with beautiful bracelets and hair ties. This way: you can see everything you own, you know where everything goes, and you know where everything ends up. Furthermore, they become really artistic elements of your room.

67.
Place a shelf over your bathroom door for the things you hardly use.

All the bathroom things you hardly need—but need in a pinch—should go on a shelf you position overtop your bathroom door. Pick out a nice shelf at your local hardware store, and attach it carefully with the provided directions. Seriously: this shelf will be your organization life-saver. You'll be able to store things you never want to see—away from everything you have to see every single day.

68.
Attach baskets to rails on your bathroom wall for enhanced bathroom organization.

This is a super-cute DIY hack that can fuel greater bathroom organization for your daily life. Simply attach three railings from top to bottom on your bathroom wall. Next, connect hooks to simple, pretty baskets. Make sure the baskets are all about the same size; you should need about six of them, two for each rail. Next, slide the hooks onto the rail with the attached baskets, and hang the baskets against the wall.

Fill one basket with rags, another with washcloths, another with toiletries, and another with hand towels, and so on. Organize them however you like, and enjoy!

69.
Create a magnetic makeup board with magnetized makeup gear.

If you're having trouble finding all your makeup in a sea of supplies, utilize this awesome DIY hack to find everything and beautify it in your dressing room. Decorate a large piece of metal with your favorite fabric, making sure to hot glue gun the fabric to the back of the metal. You can frame the metal, if you like. Next, hot glue gun small magnets to all of your favorite makeup supplies, and allow them to dry. Next, position the makeup supplies on the metal, and arrange them beautifully. Head back to the magnetized board every time you want to find your makeup!

70.
Hang a ladder from your ceiling to hang your wet clothes.

Do you have trouble finding a place to hang your drying clothes during laundry day? If yes, you should absolutely hang a ladder from your ceiling. It's really artistic looking, you can paint it however you like, and it's the perfect idea to hang your clothes. To do it, all you have to do is:

A. Paint a five-foot ladder however you please. Hang small hooks from the ladder handles for greater hanging ease.

B. Attach chains to both sides of the ladder, and attach the chains to the ceiling to hang the ladder horizontally—at an appropriate height so that you don't smack your head.

C. Hang up your clothes on either the hooks or the handles, and enjoy!

71.
Store your children's balls with bungee cords.

When your garage seems like an overwhelming mess of children's balls, you know you need to make some alterations to make everything come together better. To do this, utilize some bungee cords, some shelves, and some drilled holes.

A. First, make sure there is a shelf at the bottom of the garage wall and a shelf about five feet directly above the bottom shelf. Utilize whatever shelves you can construct. Just make sure there's area for the bungee cords to "grab" onto.

B. Next, drill three holes, evenly spaced apart, through both of the shelves. Try to make sure that the holes align from top to bottom.

C. Strap the bungee cords from bottom shelf to the top shelf to create an "interior" area in which you can keep the balls without allowing them to escape.

D. Utilize as many bungee cords and as many drilled holes as your particular ball collection requires.

72.
Hang your sports gear on a pegboard.

Again: your garage is still a mess, even after the awesome DIY ball storage hack listed above. Position a pegboard in your garage in order to fuel better organization into your garage life. Do this by hammering it into your wall. Next, hang hooks in the pegboard, and hang your helmets, your bike tires, your hockey sticks, your ball bags, your tennis rackets—everything—from this pegboard.

73.
Create a Mason jar organizer for your screws.

If you have a hard time finding your screws, your nails—and all the right sizes for both, you should look into this awesome Mason jar organization shelf. Do this by gluing Mason jar lids onto the bottom of a shelf, equidistant from each other. Next, after it dries, attach this shelf to a pegboard or your garage wall. Put your different sizes of screws and nails into separate Mason jars, and then screw the Mason jars into their lids. This way, you can keep everything separate—and the jars look really interesting and pretty hanging from the wooden shelf.

74.
Look to a clean dustpan for this essential household hack.

When you can't fill up large containers because they can't fit in your sink, what do you do? This cleaning and household hack is perfect for you. Simply place a completely clean dustpan—one with a tunnel-like handle—in the sink. Run the water from the trough to the handle and out through the spout to pour into your large container on the floor. This way, you are filling your container without making a huge mess!

75.
Cover up wooden dings in your furniture with this natural hack.

When you ding up your wooden furniture, there's not a lot you can do. It just ends up looking used and disgusting, doesn't it? Well, this unique hack leaves you with natural-looking wooden furniture once more. Simply utilize a walnut and rub the walnut over the parts of the wood you wish to clean up. It works instantly!

76.
Hold your place in a roll of tape with a bread tab.

Your life is wasted constantly looking for the end of the tape, isn't it? If you always hold your place with a bread tab, however, you can find the tape, use the tape, and put the tape away with an efficiency unrivaled by anything else. This is especially important if you don't have fingernails. Guys, I'm looking at you.

77.
Hold a nail with a clothespin.

If you can't quite grasp a nail with your fingers—I'm looking at you, girls—you should look to this unique hack to keep your nail in place when you're hammering away. Simply position your nail where you want it and seal it with the clothespin. Then, as you hold the clothespin, you can nail the nail into the wall. Voila!

78.
Wrap a rubber band around a paint can vertically.

When you're painting, you usually need something to wipe the excess pain off with, don't you? This hack gets the job done. Simply wrap a rubber band around your paint jar so that the strip crosses exactly in the middle of the paint container. That way, you can run the bristles over the rubber band and then get to work painting once more without drips!

79.
Use toilet paper rolls to keep wrapping paper under wraps.

Wrapping paper can really come to pieces throughout the off-months. To keep it in check, slice open a toilet paper roll and slip the roll over your wrapping paper. That way: the wrapping paper won't slide all over the place or crumple. Furthermore, you're finding a useful thing to do with your toilet paper rolls!

Chapter 2:
DIY Crafts and Parenting Hacks

No one's ever said the phrase "easy parenting" and meant it. However, with the following DIY Parenting Hacks, little things come together in an impressive way. You start to LOOK like you know what you're doing—even if you don't.

1.
Give your children their own personalized, designated cup with attached magnets.

If your children are always leaving their cups around the house, allow them to choose one cup that is, forevermore, THEIRS. Attach magnets to the cup and ask them to stick it to the refrigerator between uses. (If your fridge is not magnetic, find a convenient place to put up a magnetic strip.) This way: you only have to clean one cup from each child, forevermore! Plus, they'll always know where to retrieve it when they want some water.

2.
Place oilcloth over your kids' outdoor picnic table.

So often outdoor picnic tables become a little soggy during a rainstorm. If you simply hot glue gun some oilcloth to your child's outdoor picnic table, the water will glide right off instead of making a puddle.

Hot glue gun the oilcloth to the bottom of the seats and the top of the picnic table and wrap the edges around to meet on the bottom. This way, it won't come unsealed up top.

3.
Put Capri Suns in the freezer.

If your kids want a new take on an old snack, simply place Capri Suns in the freezer. When you remove them, cut them across the top and allow your kids to eat them with a spoon. The Capri Sun transforms into a slush, and it's delicious!

4.
Choose a sticker to cut in half, placing one half in one shoe, and another half in the other shoe.

Your young children probably have a difficult time distinguishing between their right and left shoes. Put some ease into their life with this awesome parenting hack. Choose a cute "face" sticker, and cut the face down the middle—so that two large eyes peer out from the bottom of the shoes. Place one half in one shoe, against the inner sole, and the other half in the other shoe, against the inner sole. That way, when the shoes are paired right, they create a "face."

5.
Use clean restaurant sauce containers for your pacifiers.

So often, pacifiers become mussed up in your purse by accident. In order to keep everything clean and sanitary, start placing pacifiers in your used and cleaned sauce containers from to-go restaurants. This way, you can seal up your pacifiers until you need them!

6.
Create this mix to remove stubborn baby food stains from a onesie.

Onesie set-in stains can really be a bummer: especially since those things are so cute! In order to alleviate this worry, simply mix together 1 tbsp. of baking soda, ½ cup of hydrogen peroxide, and 1 tbsp. of Dawn dish soap. Stir well, and pour the creation over the stain. Allow it to sit for 30 minutes, and then rinse the onesie to remove the stain.

7.
Fill water balloons with a used soap dispenser.

After the soap has left your soap dispenser, you can easily refurbish the dispenser to fill up your water balloons. Simply add water to the soap dispenser and attach the end of the balloon to the dispenser. Squirt the water into the balloon evenly, one dash at a time, and fill the balloon lightly—making sure not to overfill. They become the perfect "weapons" in a kids' play fight.

8.
Write a message on your child's arm and seal it with a liquid bandage.

When you go out in public, you need a way for your child to be found if you lose him. (Not that you will. But the fear is constantly present, isn't it?) In order to do this, simply write on your child's forearm: your name, the child's name, and your number. Then, position a liquid bandage over the writing in order to seal it.

9.
Place a visible sign where kids should cut the toilet paper to reduce waste.

Your child probably uses too much toilet paper. It's engrained in children's brains to waste—and toilet paper is no different. If you place a bright sticker or notecard that says something like: STOP, your child will know when to cut the paper off. Pretty cool, no?

10.
Rubber band for pencil gripping.

If your child is having a difficult time gripping his pencil during his beginning writing stages, try this creative hack. Wrap a rubber band around his wrist. Then, twist the rubber band once, and wrap this newly formed circle around a pencil as he grips it. This allows him to hold onto the pencil better and keep the rubber band in place as he writes.

11.
Place an essential oil on kids' cuts.

Accident-prone children are bound to have a few bruises and cuts along the way. Therefore, it's essential that you look to this awesome essential oil, helichrysum, to heal their cuts and bruises properly. Simply portion out a bit of the essential oil over your clean fingers, and rub the oil over the cut. Do this every few hours, and the cut should begin to heal soundly in a few hours.

12.
Create faux tap dancing shoes for an excited child.

Your children probably want to dance and sing all day long; and why shouldn't they? Help them out on their way to stage and screen by gluing pennies to the back and front of the sole of an old pair of their shoes. This way, they can tap this way and that on your solid-surface floors with ease.

13.
Place a "safe" sticker on your car for errands.

So: when you go to the gas station or you head somewhere to unload the car and your children get out of the car with you because, of course, they're naturally curious, it's probably natural to feel that they'll wander off somewhere. In order to alleviate this worry, simply position a "safe" sticker on your car. While your children are outside with you, they MUST keep their hands on this sticker. Make a game of it. This way, you can always know where they are, and they can always know where to stand.

14.
Handle sparklers with a red plastic cup.

Red Solo Cups just got a whole lot safer than they were at college parties. If you put a round hole in the very center bottom of the cup, you can stick a sparkler through it. Allow your young children to place their hands inside the cup and grab the safe end of the sparkler as you light the other side. They can watch and dance with the sparkler without burning themselves.

15.
Inflate an outdoor pool inside for a safe area to play.

If you go somewhere without a designated playpen—or you don't want to invest in one—simply utilize an outdoor pool. If you blow it up and place it in your living room, position pillows and blankets on the bottom, and arrange all your toddler's favorite toys inside, the pool becomes the perfect playpen.

16.
Add 2 tbsp. of fabric softener and water to a spray bottle for hairspray for a doll.

If your daughter's dolls need a serious hairdo makeover, simply bring together fabric softener and water in a very small spray bottle. Spray the doll's hair with the mixture, and allow it to sit for two minutes. Afterwards, brush through the doll's hair to reveal stunning shine.

17.
Place glue gun glue in the holes of bath toys.

So often, children's bath toys can get moldy when too much water collects inside of them. In order to plug up those holes, simply glue the small holes in the toys with the glue gun and allow them to dry. This eliminates the risk of mold and brings added safety to your child's playtime.

18.
Bring shower caddies from the dollar store for Happy Meals and eating in the car.

If you children are messy eaters, never fear. If you bring super-cheap shower caddies into the car with you, you can align their meals in the shower caddies and allow your children to eat easily—without tossing plates on the floor. Furthermore, there's a perfect drink location for them to utilize so that they don't spill their milk!

19.
Place a crib sheet over a playpen when your baby is outside.

When your baby is outside with you, you'll want to protect her from any bugs or mosquitos as she plays away. To do this, simply drape a crib sheet over the top of the playpen. Furthermore, this protects your baby from the sun—which is really important in these beginning months, as you know.

20.
Utilize an egg carton for greater card game organization.

If you and your children love to play card games—but it gets a bit confusing sometimes because they're too little to be organized—consider utilizing an egg carton. Do this by cutting off the bottom part of an egg carton, and slicing each of the egg holders in the very center for card holders. Allow your children to slide the cards into the slits to see everything—without holding every card and losing track.

21.
Create no-slick shoes with a glue gun.

If you put small dots on the bottom of your children's shoes, they won't go slip-sliding away the next time they step on a squeaky clean surface. The floor will have something to grab onto, and your children will be able to rush around everywhere they please, without worrying. (Note that you won't have to worry, either.)

22.
Separate your children's different clothing with the "dot" method.

If you can't quite keep your children's clothing apart, simply put one dot for one child, two dots for the second child, three dots for the third child, etc. Place the dots on the tags of the clothes. That way, as you leaf through the clothes on laundry day, you know which pile is for whom.

23.
Create a to-do creativity wallet for your kids at restaurants.

My kids have serious trouble staying still at the restaurant table. That's why I created a wallet with pens, pencils, stickers, and drawing paper. My kids love leafing through the wallet, choosing their favorite pieces of paper to draw on, and playing with the stickers. I never leave home without it, just in case.

24.
When you make frozen pops, add some Jell-O so they don't melt.

Frozen pops can be a huge catastrophe if you have children. If you're making an awesome at-home, natural pops recipe, however, it's essential that you mix in about ½ pack of Jell-O (whichever flavor you choose). That way, the popsicles won't melt everywhere, and your children won't be sticky messes.

25.
Always take a small baby bath to your beach.

When you head to the beach, it's important to prepare by bringing a small baby bath with you. That way, your baby can have a rollicking adventure in her "small ocean," while you and the rest of your family have a rollicking adventure in the big one. (Make sure, of course, that someone stays with the baby at all times.) Furthermore, this is important to use so that your baby doesn't get overheated.

26.
Utilize a super-cheap camera bag for a diaper bag.

All the compartments of a super-cheap camera bag from your local thrift store create your essential diaper bag. Creams, diapers, wipes—whatever!—come together in this once-artistic bag. What's more? They're trendy and easy to carry around from place to place.

27.
Place a padlock in the hole of your electric plugs.

So often, you hear horror stories about children placing electric plugs into outlets and becoming electrocuted. However, you can halt that right now by putting a padlock in the hole of your electric plug. That way, your child will be unable to position the plug in the wall, keeping his little fingers away from the electric outlet. Furthermore, the plug will be a reminder to your children to stay away from the things! They're off-limits.

28.
Place a puppy pad beneath your child's fitted sheet.

Save your mattress from your child's wet bed accidents by placing a puppy pad beneath your child's fitted sheet. This creates an essential time-saver. After all: you won't have to wash the mattress over and over again. You'll just have to toss away the puppy pad, wash some sheets, and regroup for next time. (This is, after all, a troubling time for all.)

29.
Place your baby or toddler in a laundry basket in the bathtub so they don't lose their toys.

The bathtub is a scary place for your child. Keep everything contained for them by placing a very young child in a laundry basket in the tub. That way, their toys are always in reaching distance and they're able to bounce around without falling down in the water.

30.
Always ask the baby his or her name— whether or not the baby can talk yet.

Gender faux pas are NO fun, especially between parents. If you meet a parent and a baby or toddler in the street, always lean down and ask the baby his or her name. The parent will probably answer with something that clears things up: "Her name is—" etc. That way, you don't have to guess, and you can get the conversation going a bit faster.

31.
Keep your tossed-out cell phones and allow your children to play with them.

When your kids are armed with "new" technology, they can begin to learn about the world around them. This is going to be essential moving forward: when technology is all the world is! Furthermore, they can take fun pictures and learn to become artistic. How fun is that?

32.
Strengthen your child's upper body with the monkey bars: read on.

If you ask your child to spend some more time on the monkey bars, you'll see enhanced results in his or her handwriting. When you strengthen your child's upper body, his fine or her motor skills strengthen, as well. This leads to better handwriting which ultimately leads to better communication in the world!

33.
Also add sprinkles.

Seriously: even if what you're giving your child is super-healthy—in juice or smoothie form—sprinkle on a few colorful sugar dots for emphasis. Everything in the world CAN be fun and bright. It can. Allow your child to think that way, as well.

34.
Create a fake hammock with a large blanket and a table.

If you want to have a place for your kids to "hang out," simply tie a large blanket around your table, with the tie at the top. Leave some extra slack at the bottom to allow your child to hang in. This provides a super-fun, jungle-like environment. Plus: kids love hiding, they love swinging, and they love being under stuff. This fits the bill.

35.
Always trace your child's feet for solo shoe shopping.

Your kid's feet change every single day. If you trace your children's feet with a crayon on a piece of paper, you can take your paper along with you the next time you go shopping, you can suit them up with a brand new pair of shoes—without them whining and complaining. A few minutes to yourself is essential, don't you think?

36.
Tie up a tank top with a barrette.

If your little girl's tank top straps are all over the place, revealing a little too much skin on a hot day, you can tie the strap together on her upper back utilizing a pretty barrette. This way: her shirt is in check, she has an added accessory, and you don't have to worry about her. Phew!

37.
Place vapor rub on your children's feet to stop coughing.

Yep. It's essential that you stop your children's nighttime coughing to allow them to sleep better. (After all, they're super-crabby in the morning when they haven't been sleeping.) If you rub their feet with vapor rub and then place socks on their feet, their cough will immediately lessen. It should be gone in just a few days!

38.
Create a faux-monster spray to spray in your scared child's room.

So much of childhood is being scared and creating stories in your head. You can relieve your child's fear by creating this awesome "monster" spray. It can be just a bit of water—or some good-smelling essential oils. Pour the stuff in a spray bottle, and then decorate the spray bottle, writing "monster spray" on it. Spray the spray in children's rooms before they go to sleep to alleviate their rushing minds.

39.
Place a single wad of Kleenex beneath your child's two last fingers for proper pencil holding.

If your child is having a difficult time holding his pencil, you should learn this essential DIY hack. Simply roll up a wad of Kleenex and stuff it beneath your child's two last fingers. Place the pencil in his hand—the right way—and force him to maintain the correct form with this technique. It really works!

40.
Place a pool noodle on a door for a doorstopper.

Your toddler has no self-control, does he? (Of course, a lot of this is muscle-based.) In order to alleviate his lack of control, simply slice a pool noodle vertically, and position the pool noodle along the door. This way, the door won't slam, your baby won't get woken up, and nobody will get locked out. Phew. Keep this thing with you at all times—or have one positioned everywhere around your house.

41.
Place a maxi pad in a potty-training kid's diaper during the nighttime.

If your child is in the potty-training phase, place the maxi pad in their diaper to relieve them from soaked pajamas. This way: there's a double layer keeping them from discomfort. You'll get through this phase—even if you have to shed a few tears along the way. Good luck!

42.
Glitz up your money to make it look like it's from the tooth fairy.

How magical is tooth fairy money? So magical. You made that tooth in your body, and now you're getting paid for it. Glitz up your kid's tooth fairy money to enhance their experience. Place some glue-glitter on top in a decorative design, and stick the dried glitter dollar (or two) beneath his or her pillow. So fun!

43.
Place a stability ball beneath your children when they're doing homework.

Recent studies have shown that when children sit on stability balls—rather than chairs—they have a greater ability to concentrate when they do homework or try to read. Furthermore, this will help them strengthen their back, their core, and their legs as they work. Cool! (This works for you, as well, if you're interested.)

44.
Place formula or milk in an ice cube tray, and freeze a pacifier on top.

When your baby begins his teething process, he'll be in a load of pain—and you'll feel the pain, as well, in the form of sadness for your aching baby. In order to alleviate your baby's gums, simply freeze a pacifier in an ice cube tray filled with milk or formula. After the stuff has frozen over the pacifier, remove the pacifier with the attached formula or milk and give it to your baby. Your baby will love the soothing feeling.

45.
Give a baby medicine with this one cool hack.

Your baby probably doesn't want you to drip-drop any medicine in his mouth. (Not without freaking out, that is.) In order to deliver drip medicine to your baby, you can cut a small hole in the very center of a pacifier. Give the pacifier to your baby, and then dribble the medicine through the pacifier to allow it to drip through the hole.

46.
Create a faux hair tie with a zip tie.

If you're out of pony tail holders—and all you have is this zip tie, you can hold a girl's hair up with some zip ties. It's not the most attractive look in the world, of course. However, sometimes it's essential to get that mane out of your young girl's face.

47.
Create a coloring travel kit with an old DVD case.

Your old DVD cases can come in handy with this artistic hack. Remove all mention of the movie from the DVD case. Next, position bits of blank paper on the left side of the inside of the case—

where the "information" section used to go. Then, position colored pencils on the right side, forming a "holder" with a bit of cut folder, taped together to fit the inside of the DVD case. Now, you have everything you need for a traveling art case!

48.
Bring a shower caddy on a long road trip.

When you strap a shower caddy to the back of your front seat of your car, your child—in the back seat—can store all of his favorite things: from his snacks to his toys to his books. This awesome hack is perfect for you, as well. You can reach around and grab your map right where you put it or find the book you're reading when it's not your turn to drive. Furthermore, it provides easy cleanup when you arrive at your destination.

49.
Allow your kids to eat messy snacks while they're in the bathtub.

Your kids LOVE messy snacks: think s'mores, melted chocolate, peanut butter-based things. However, when they eat them in real life, they're a mess afterwards. If you give them the snacks while they're in the bathtub, they'll love them just as much. Maybe more: since they're naked and eating chocolate.

50.
Create DIY sock grips so your kids don't go flying on hardwood floors.

Place small dots of fabric paint on the bottom of your children's socks. That way, they won't go flying all over the place when they rush around your house. Furthermore, your kids won't hurt themselves, and they'll love the interesting dots on the bottom of their socks. This hack is so easy, you can literally do it for each of your children's socks.

51.
Color scuffed shoes with crayon.

Crayon is oil-based and therefore super-awesome for touching up your kids' scuffed shoes. When your kids come home with material missing from their shoes, you can simply color them in utilizing a dark crayon—or a crayon that matches the color of the shoe. This way, your children's shoes look awesome from far away, and you don't have to buy new shoes every single week.

52.
Create "bed rails" in the hotel.

When you go on vacation, you might worry that your children will fall out of the bed without their usual rail system. However, if you create rails through this useful hack, you'll have no worry at all. Simply roll pillows directly beneath the fitted sheet on all edges of the large bed. Your children will be unable to fall down and hit their heads on the ground.

53.
Allow your very young children to play with play dough–while it's wrapped up.

So often, toddlers stick things in their mouth, swallow things, and get into really big messes. That's why, so often, they aren't allowed to play with play dough—even when it's super-fun! Allow them to play by placing the play dough in a zip-lock bag. They can mess around with the play dough, squish it around, without becoming huge play dough slobs. Phew.

54.
Place a crazy straw in a cup upside down.

Your kids are constant spill-creating disasters. However, when you place a crazy straw in the cup upside down, your kids will be unable to remove the straw from the cup. When you do this, the drink will ultimately rest in its cup—instead of ending up all over your carpet. Feels good to be a genius, doesn't it?

55.
Slice an apple-and then put it back together.

When packing your kids' lunch, you'll of course slice their apple for them. But then, when they go to eat the apple, it'll be brown! In order to scrap this disaster, simply position the apple back together and secure it with rubber bands. Teach children to take the rubber bands off carefully and enjoy their crisp apples.

56.
Use a pizza cutter for easy small food cutting!

How often have you labored over your child's food, slicing and dicing away with a knife and fork? Rid yourself of that disaster with this awesome hack. Simply roll away at the food with a small pizza cutter, and create small bite-sized pieces for your child to easily munch on. Delicious!

57.
If your child hates the shirt she or he is wearing-

How often is your morning interrupted by a screaming child because he or she doesn't like the design of whatever shirt you've chosen for him or her? Okay. Take a deep breath. This is an easy hack. Simply put on the shirt backwards. Your child won't know the difference, you can still go on your way, and no one is hurt.

58.
Remove permanent marker marks on wood with white toothpaste.

When your child takes to the wood with permanent marker, you probably think all is lost. However, if you utilize cheap white toothpaste on the lines, allow it to sit for 15 minutes, and then scrub at it with a bit of water and a washcloth, the stuff will come off! Phew.

59.
Place a coffee cup lid beneath a frozen pop for easy cleanup.

Your kids LOVE frozen pops. It's something that we've already covered in this very book, actually. However, the pops are a super-mess. If you stick the bottom of the frozen pop's handle through the hole in your coffee cup lid and allow your child to grasp the handle beneath, licking away as she does this, your lid can soak up all the gross mess. Easy! (Just make sure your child doesn't spill the drippings.)

60.
Place peas in the pasta shells.

If your toddler or super-picky eater won't eat—anything—liven up his or her meal with this awesome hack. Simply cook the peas and the pasta shells, and then place the pea inside the shell. Tell your child that the peas are actually pearls. If you liven up the magic of your child's meal, he or she will be much more likely to eat up!

61.
Place a large, opened cardboard box over your steps.

Create your own slide with this awesome hack. Simply open the cardboard box and place it on your steps, from one landing to the bottom. Allow your kids to slide down the steps easily, landing in a pile of pillows at the bottom. How fun is that?

62.
"Play video games" with your children with this fun hack.

When you want to play video games AND interact with your children, give your kids controllers that aren't connected. That way: you can play, they can watch you play, and they can feel like they're a part of the awesome action. Note that you shouldn't do this for too long, as the screen can be bad for the children's eyes.

63.
Easily remove a splinter DIY.

When your kids have a pesky splinter, you can remove it easily with this awesome hack. Simply mix together a bit of baking soda and water and place the mixture over your child's splinter. Amuse your child during this time while you wait. Sing songs; play a game; whatever. The mixture will help the splinter to pop out of the child's skin, leaving you to just pick up the pieces and move on.

64.
Create a fun bracelet with your phone number for your child to wear.

When you head out into public, it's essential that your child is somehow "marked" to be yours. Do this in a fun and creative way by creating a bracelet with your number on it. That way, if you somehow get separated from your child, whoever finds him or her can call you instantly and bring you your child.

65.
Spray hot seat belt buckles with a water spray bottle.

Remember how hot the seat belt buckles get in the middle of the summer, ultimately burning your children's small fingers? To avoid this, always keep a spray bottle in your car. Before they touch the buckles, spray the buckles with the water. The evaporation immediately cools the metal and the plastic. Note that the water does not need to be cold for this to occur.

66.
Place pool noodles on every "chain" of your trampoline.

Those chains all around the trampoline are pretty scary-looking. When your kids inevitably land on them, it doesn't feel good. Create a cushion around your trampoline with old pool noodles. Do this by slicing them, length-wise, so that you create a slit. Easily form the pool noodle around the chain, making sure that it's the correct length for the chain. Alternate the colors for fun flair, and enjoy!

67.
Remove strawberry stems with a straw.

If you don't want to tote around a knife for your next picnic, this essential fruit hack is perfect to keep things safe. Your child can even do it! Simply push the straw through the bottom of a strawberry and push the stem off the top: pop! Your kids will love doing it, and they will LOVE the super-healthy snack it accompanies.

68.
Create throwaway plates with your pizza box.

The next time you and your family order a pizza, simply tear away at the cardboard in order to create small, personalized plates for your kids. This way, they can be as messy as they want and simply toss the plate into the trashcan. You won't have to work hard after dinner, and your house will look like dinner never happened.

Chapter 3: DIY Cleaning and Organizing Hacks

Chances are, you're probably spending too much time cleaning your kitchen, your bathroom, your living room, and every other element of your house. You're ready to get away from the scrub brush, get out of the bathroom, and start living your life! However, in order to do that, you need to start elevating your DIY game with these awesome cleaning hacks.

1.
Remove oil from your stovetop with extra oil.

All the extra oil and grease buildup on your stovetop can be eliminated with oil. Simply drop a few dribbles of whatever oil you utilize—vegetable oil, olive oil—on the grease stain. Rub at it with paper towel. This will get the gunk up easily—without harsh chemicals.

2.
Remove microfiber couch stains with rubbing alcohol.

When you get stains on your super-nice microfiber couch, don't worry. They can come off really easy with this cleaning hack. Pour rubbing alcohol into your spray bottle, and spray the area of the stain. Next, rub at the area with the stain with a white sponge. Next, allow the area to dry. When it completely dries, rub at the area with a bristle brush in order to realign the fibers to create your stunning couch once more.

3.
Shine and cleanse your stovetop with car wax.

The wax that you can utilize to make your car shine can also help your stove—the central piece of your kitchen—burst with light. Place car wax on your stovetop and then wipe it off with a paper towel to create a brand-new-looking stove top. Furthermore, future spills will clean up much more easily if you do this wax treatment every few days.

4.
Place vinegar on a sock to clean the blinds.

The blinds can really accumulate dust and lead to enhanced allergens and a musty stench in your home. In order to cleanse them, simply mix together one part vinegar for one part water. Next, dip a sock into the mixture and rub it onto the blinds—with your hand in the sock. Utilize another sock in order to wipe away the mixture. Next, clean the socks in the washing machine, and do this every few weeks for ready cleanliness.

5.
Cleanse your burners–without scrubbing.

When your stove burners are really gunky, simply place each of them in a separate Ziploc bag. Next, place one-third cup ammonia in each of the bags, as well. Place the bags outside in a place far away from where your kids hang out. Allow them to sit outside for twelve hours before removing the stove burners, wiping them down, and placing them back on the stovetop. Super easy!

6.
Remove water rings with a blow dryer.

The water rings that litter your wooden coffee tables all over your house can be eliminated once and for all with this awesome cleaning hack. Before forcing everyone to start utilizing coasters, take a blow dryer with you throughout the house and hold the blow dryer on HIGH next to the rings. The rings will disappear in just about three minutes.

7.
Pull up a carpet stain with an iron.

Carpet stains come from everywhere: from everyone in your family, from guests, from pets. Everywhere. And in order to rid your carpet of carpet stains, you can follow this super-easy DIY trick. Simply mix together 2 parts water with 1 part vinegar. Stir well, and spray the mixture onto your carpet stain. Next, place a bit of water on a clean rag, and place the rag over the stain. Next, place the iron on the rag and steam it for about 30 seconds. After you remove the iron and the rag, the stain should now be on the rag—rather than the carpet.

8.
Remove oil from the carpet with this awesome hack.

When oil spills on your carpet, all is not lost. Begin by sprinkling baking soda over the area and allowing it to sit there, soaking up the oil, for about 15 minutes. Next, vacuum the soda from the carpet. In a separate container, mix together about two cups of warm water, 1 tbsp. of vinegar, and 1 tbsp. of clear dishwasher liquid. Apply this mixture to the oil, as well, and allow it to sit on the carpet for five minutes. Next, remove the liquid with a dampened sponge, and enjoy your super-clean carpet!

9.
Wipe down stainless steel with lemon.

Create an easy cleanup with this awesome bathroom hack. Simply slice a lemon into two pieces and rub the stainless steel stains on your sink and faucet with the lemon. The lemon will immediately relieve hard water stains and rust. Furthermore, this is perfect if you don't want to utilize chemicals!

10.
Make a natural tub cleanser.

If you don't want to utilize harsh chemicals when cleaning your bathtub—especially if you have little ones around—you should definitely look to this awesome natural hack. Simply mix together 1 tsp. liquid soap with 5 drops peppermint essential oil. Next, mix in 1 cup of baking soda. Stir well, and add water to create a paste. Add the paste to the bottom of the bathtub and scrub lightly. Wipe the mixture with water, and rinse well.

11.
Clean up your cast iron pots.

Cast iron cleaning can be a bit difficult. However, if you utilize coarse salt to clean them, this can go very smoothly. Simply add the coarse salt to the bottom of the cash iron pot or skillet and add a few drops of water. Scrub at the salt with a sponge in order to remove all residue and oil. Afterwards, rinse the pot and dry it completely to prevent all rusting.

12.
Steam up a microwave to clean it.

Do this awesome DIY hack when you need to clean an offensive microwave mess. Simply add 2 cups of water, 2 tbsp. of vinegar and 2 drops of peppermint essential oil to a microwave-safe bowl. Place the bowl in the microwave, and microwave the bowl for five minutes on HIGH. Afterwards, remove the bowl, and wipe down the inside of the microwave with a paper towel. This hack is super-important—especially if you rely on your microwave for a ton of meals.

13.
Vinegar in the coffee pot for cleansing.

Your coffee maker is rife with disgusting odors and stains. Pour water and vinegar through your coffee maker as if you were "brewing" coffee. This vinegar will relieve your coffee maker of buildup. After half of the coffee making cycle, halt the coffee maker in its tracks to allow it to rest with the vinegar inside. Then, allow the coffee maker to finish its cycle. Cleanse the coffee maker with a few rounds of simple water.

14.
Cream of tartar for stainless steel toaster oven.

Your stainless steel toaster oven is rife with stains. Not to worry: you can utilize cream of tartar for ready cleaning. Simply place 1 tbsp. of cream of tartar with about 4 tbsp. of water. You should create a milk-like mixture. Next, rub this creation over the stains. Allow it to sit for one minute before wiping your toaster oven clean.

15.
Cleanse your toilet with duct tape and vinegar.

Your toilet is the menacing figure in your life: you don't want to touch it, you don't want to clean it, and yet—there it is, waiting for you. Clean it correctly with this awesome DIY technique.

    A. Begin by turning off the water to your toilet.

    B. Next, empty the entire tank of the toilet.

    C. Make sure to seal up the toilet siphon jets with duct tape.

    D. Next, pour an entire gallon of the vinegar into the toilet's tank. Flush the toilet and allow the vinegar to head to the rim. The duct tape will hold the vinegar there.

    E. Allow this situation to rest overnight.

    F. Remove the duct tape and brush at the surface of the toilet with a toilet brush. Allow the tank to fill with water once more, and flush the toilet once more to remove all the vinegar.

16.
Clean your windowsills with vinegar and Q-tips.

The windows get an even washing all the time. However, the dirt and build-up that accumulates in your windowsill is actually unbelievable, lending more and more dirt to your already cleaned windows. Next time you clean your windows, utilize this easy DIY hack to clean your windowsill, as well. Simply dip the cotton part of the Q-tip into some pure vinegar and wipe at the dirt in the "inserts" of your windowsill. As you pull the grime from the inside of the windowsill, wipe at whatever comes out with a rag. Continue up the windowsill.

17.
Cleanse your computer keyboard with a toothbrush.

The dust and sticky stuff that builds up on your keyboard can leave your keyboard utterly useless. Luckily, this cleaning hack is super-easy and essential for better keyboard longevity. Simply unplug your keyboard from any electric outlet. Next, utilize an old toothbrush to dust between the keys and on top of the keys.

18.
Utilize the top of a ketchup bottle to make "suction" on your vacuum.

If you often vacuum in hard-to-reach places, this cleaning hack is essential for you. You'll need to find an old-fashioned plastic ketchup lid—like the ones in a condiment set with a long, thin tube at the top. If the top is used, you'll want to completely cleanse it. Next, place the lid on the top of your vacuum's hose with duct tape. With this awesome DIY hack, you can completely cleanse your home—down to the smallest corners—once and for all.

19.
Look to white chalk for greasy stains.

If you have grease stains on your clothes, don't pop them in the washing machine too soon. Instead, you'll want to take to those stains with something very, very unlikely: white chalk. When you rub the chalk over the clothing stain, the chalk actually absorbs the grease from your clothes. Allow the chalk to sit on your clothes for a few hours before tossing your clothes in the laundry and living a carefree life!

20.
Don't scrub your shower heads: use this DIY hack.

If you want to clean your showerheads, don't bother to scrub and scrub at the scum build-up. Instead, you should utilize this awesome trick overnight when no one wants to use the showerhead, anyway. Simply bring white vinegar into a medium-sized plastic bag. Tie the bag around the shower head, making sure to hold it securely in place at the showerhead's "neck." Allow this to sit there for about twelve hours. Afterwards, remove the plastic bag, run water out of the showerhead, and see all the gunk depart from the showerhead instantly.

21.
Clean up your wall's baseboards with dryer sheets.

Your white baseboards all over your house seem to accumulate the most dirt daily, don't they? This forces you to clean them all the time. However, with this awesome hack, you can completely cleanse your boards whenever you like for lifelong cleanliness. Simply utilize a dryer sheet to dust at the baseboards. This technique forces the boards to completely repel the dust.

22.
Remove unwanted clothes with this awesome hack.

You know you should get rid of your clothes every so often: but how do you know which clothes to get rid of? Use this awesome Oprah-inspired hack to get to the root of your clothing problems. Simply hang your hangers in your closet "backwards," with the pointer forcing out, toward you. When you utilize a clothing item, place the hanger the proper way in your closet. After about six months, you can understand which clothing items you DO wear and which ones you don't. This way, you can get rid of the ones you don't need!

23.
Strip off unwanted pot and pan stains with apple peels.

If your pots and pans have unwanted stains—and all stains are unwanted, after all—you could scrub and scrub at them. However, if you utilize this awesome DIY hack, you can completely remove those stains super easily. Simply peel an apple, toss the apple peels into your pan or pot, add water on top of the apple peels, and allow the water to simmer for 35 minutes. Afterwards, pour out the water and cleanse the pot with a swift wipe of your rag.

24.
Clip your car freshener to your central AC unit.

Rather than investing in expensive household sprays, you can utilize this awesome cleaning hack to keep your house smelling fresh and clean. Simply clip your car freshener to your central AC unit and get the breeze blowing. This fuels the fresh smells into every area of your home!

25.
Mix together baking soda and bleach to cleanse your house of grout mold.

Grout mold accumulates as the years go by. Pretty soon, you find yourself backed into an unfortunate corner with grout mold on your hands. Luckily, if you mix together about one-half cup of baking soda to each 1 cup of bleach, you can create an awesome recipe to cleanse your home of grout mold. Be careful and wear gloves when applying the recipe to the grout mold. If you scrub at it, allow it to sit for a few minutes, and then cleanse the grout mold from the tiles, you will find beautiful shine in the once grimy location.

26.
Create homemade Febreze with this awesome recipe.

If your life is a constant string of smells, you won't want to go out and buy a new Febreze every few days. You'll go broke! Instead, make this super-frugal recipe for your homemade Febreze.

    A. Combine together 1 tbsp. fabric softener, 2 tbsp. baking soda, 8 drops lavender essential oil, and warm water to the top of a small spray bottle.

    B. Mix together the above ingredients together in that spray bottle, and then spray the faux Febreze wherever the bad winds take you.

27.
Utilize a lime and some baking soda to clean your sink.

When your sink is a stinking mess, look to this everyday hack to clean your sink and reap the rewards of remarkable shine. Simply pour baking soda into the bottom of a bowl. Next, slice a lime in half, and dip one of the lime faces into the baking soda. Scrub at your sink and your faucet with the lime, making sure to remove the juices with pressure. Continue to dip into the baking soda as needed. Enjoy the citrus-shine of your brand-new sink!

28.
Always put a cheap kind of soap in your pretty "foam" soap dispensers.

In the beginning, you bought a pretty foam soap dispenser. You won't want to continue buying new foam soap dispensers in the future. However, you can recreate the magic with this awesome hack. Simply add super-cheap soap to the dispenser and then add a bit of water to the hand soap. This allows it to foam up appropriately and fuel your love of luxury.

29.
Remove sticker residue from your jars and cans with this hack.

If you want to reuse jars and cans—but you can't get the sticky stuff off the sides—look to this awesome hack. You won't even know the sticky stuff was ever even there! Simply melt 2 tbsp. of coconut oil in a pan. After it begins to melt, add an equal amount of baking soda and stir well. Add this mixture to wherever your gunk is, and scrub at it for a few moments to remove it. The gunk should strip up easily.

30.
Remove clothing grease stains with a bit of dish detergent.

Your dish detergent is continually rubbing grease stains off your dishes. Why, then, wouldn't it be able to remove grease stains from your clothing? Try this super-unique hack. Simply mix a bit of dish detergent with some water and then pour the mixture over your grease stain. Allow it to sit out in the air for a few hours before tossing it in the washing machine to really get the thing out. The dish detergent will have stripped the oil away from the fibers.

31.
Mix together hydrogen peroxide and flour to de-stain your granite countertops.

Your beautiful granite countertops really take a hit after constant hours of cooking, baking, and hosting. If you want to get rid of some of those super-hard granite countertop stains, look to this awesome cleaning hack. Simply mix together one part hydrogen peroxide with one part flour to create a paste. Next, add this mixture over the stains on the countertop, and allow it to sit there and harden for a few minutes before scraping it up. The paste will bring the stain up with it!

32.
Add plastic toy to the dishwasher for super-easy cleanup.

Your child's toys become really gunky and disgusting over the—well—hours. If you want to clean your child's toys after a particularly rough play date or before friends come over, you can just pop the plastic ones into the dishwasher for just a typical cycle. When they come out, they'll be shiny and new!

33.
Create homemade clothing wrinkle fighter.

If you want to remove the wrinkles from your clothes—but don't want to iron your clothes or buy super-expensive wrinkle releaser—look to this awesome hack. Bring together 32 ounces of water with 2 tbsp. of fabric softener and 2 tbsp. of isopropyl alcohol. Mix the ingredients together well in a large 2-liter bottle (that is completely cleaned, by the way), and then spray the mixture onto your wrinkled outfit (by placing a spray bottle cap on top of the 2-liter bottle). This way, your outfit is completely wrinkle-free after only a few minutes of sitting with the stuff.

34.
Fall away from paper towels and save money with this super-easy hack.

Paper towel bills can really add up—especially if you live in a messy house. I think it's really important to understand your options with regards to this problem. If you replace your paper towels with a large stack of microfiber cloths or bits and pieces of old towels, you can mop up your messes, wash your cloths, and continue to live an environmentally friendly lifestyle.

35.
Create "new" soap out of old slivers.

You know how hard it is to handle those super-small slivers of leftover soaps, correct? Often I just throw my old slivers away and make room for new soaps. However, this is very unnecessary and wasteful. If you start saving the small scraps of your old bars of soap, you can melt them all together in a small saucepan and create a new bar of soap—from a bunch of different, little ones. You can utilize this large hunk of new soap just like old soap.

    A. Simply bring all the pieces into a saucepan, turn the heat to medium-high, and start breaking up the pieces as they get hotter.

    B. Allow the mixture to boil for about five minutes, making sure that it doesn't boil over.

    C. Next, pour the mixture into a colander with a frying pan beneath so as not to lose any pieces of soap. Remove all the excess water.

    D. Pour this mixture into a glass bowl and allow it to sit out and harden together. Voila! Your new bar of soap is created.

36.
Create your own laundry soap at home.

The laundry soap bills can really add up. The most frustrating part of it all is, of course, that when you buy these laundry soaps, you're really paying for the advertising! Ugh. If you create your own soap, you'll be paying for the bare bones, and you'll be utilizing a very good product. Guaranteed.

    A. Mix together 3½ tbsp. borax, 3½ tbsp. washing soap, and 2½ tbsp. Dawn dish soap.

    B. Bring these ingredients together into a one-gallon jug, and then add 4½ cups of boiling water to the jug. Toss the mixture around in the jug until everything is mixed together, and then allow the mixture to cool. Fill the remainder of the jug with cold water, bringing the bubbles all the way to the top.

    C. Utilize this laundry soap to clean all your clothes whenever you please!

37.
Utilize olive oil to clean your makeup brushes.

Makeup brushes really accumulate the worst kind of gunk—the gunk that you ultimately have to put on your face during your rush-around hours as you ready yourself for the day ahead. In order to do this, you must gather together: olive oil, dish soap, and one dinner plate.

- A. Begin by pouring the dish soap over a dinner plate, just to coat the bottom.
- B. Next, pour olive oil over the dish soap to create a 1½ to 2 parts oil olive to dish soap ratio.
- C. Next, place your make up brush in the mixture and stir well. The makeup will begin to glide off.
- D. Afterwards, wipe the brush over your fingers to completely eliminate the makeup. This further kills all the bacteria on the brush.
- E. Place the makeup brushes on a paper towel to dry out.
- F. Afterwards, rinse the brushes in warm water, swirling them well to remove all excess "gunk."
- G. Allow the brushes to completely dry out on the paper towel.

38.
Shine up your brass with a vinegar and flour mix.

When you create this vibrant paste, you can make your brass shiny and new-looking once more—free of its past smudges. Simply mix together one part vinegar and one part flour to create a paste. Next, scrub at your brass figurines and allow the paste to harden on the brass for about five minutes. Scrub the paste off the brass to reveal the ready shine.

39.
Spray baking soda and water mixture in your oven.

When the grime in your oven become unbearable, learn this super-lazy technique to cleanse your oven easily. Mix together one cup of water with 2 tbsp. of baking soda in a spray bottle. Allow your oven to cool down, and then spray the creation over the grime. After you allow it to sit for a few minutes, utilize a sponge to wipe the grime away from your oven instantly.

40.
Make your carpet fresh: instantly.

If you're a mother with a bunch of stinky kids and animals running around your house, you probably have given your carpet up to the gods. After all: how will it ever look or smell nice again? However, this awesome cleaning hack brings essential carpet freshness back into your life. You can live a refined life once more! Simply mix together 20 drops of your favorite essential oil (I used orange) and one-third cup baking soda. Sprinkle this mixture over your odorous carpet, and then wait for four hours. Vacuum the baking soda up, and enjoy your new good-smelling carpet!

41.
Make your own window cleaner.

Window cleaner can be pretty expensive. And if you find yourself cleaning windows often—well—you should definitely look into making your own. This homemade window cleanser is perfect for at-home, at-work, or car use.

- A. Gather together ⅓ cup rubbing alcohol, ⅓ cup white vinegar, 1 tbsp. cornstarch, 2¼ cups water, 9 drops of lemon essential oil.
- B. Mix these ingredients together in a spray bottle, and shake them together.
- C. Spray the mixture onto your glass surface of choice and wipe it clean. This recipe is perfect and so cheap. You can reuse the ingredients for many, many months!

42.
Bring shine back to your stainless steel.

Your stainless steel appliances are probably streak-ridden, especially if you have a vibrant family and a lot of things happening all at once. Try out this awesome stainless steel hack. Utilize some baby oil to scrub at the streaks, wipe the baby oil clean, and reap the stunning rewards of your newly cleaned stainless steel. Yes!

43.
Hand wash your Swiffer duster.

Those expensive Swiffer dusters don't have to go to waste, after all! Simply hand wash them in the sink with a bit of warm water and a small amount of dish soap. Allow them to dry out by hanging them with your drying clothes, and enjoy the awesome benefits of continually reusable Swiffer dusters!

44.
Clean your dishwasher with this super hack.

How gross is it to think about cleaning your dishes in an already dirty dishwasher? Clean it up with this awesome hack. Place a cup of vinegar in the very top of your dishwasher and allow your dishwasher to run—completely empty except for the cup of vinegar—on its hot cycle. Afterwards, all the gunk and grime that your dishwasher has accumulated over the months will simply slide away.

45.
Clean windows and stainless steel with coffee filters.

Whenever I used to clean windows and stainless steel with regular paper towels, I would find streaks everywhere. This cleaning hack allows you to completely rid your life of needless streaks. Simply cleanse your windows and your stainless steel items with your cleaner and wipe them down with the coffee filters.

46.
Place small, easily lost items in a laundry bag and wash them in the dishwasher.

SO: all those little items you like to clean in your dishwasher—that end up lost in the bottom of your dishwasher—can be controlled with this essential cleaning hack. Place all the small things you want to clean in your dishwasher in a laundry bag. Then, place the laundry bag in the dishwasher on the top shelf and run the load through. This way: you can keep track of everything, you can easily remove everything at once, and nothing is damaged.

47.
Keep silica gel packs.

Have you ever accidentally gotten things wet that you shouldn't have? For example: have you spilled water on your iPod or dropped your phone in the toilet? If the answer is yes, you should always keep these silica gel packs with you. Silica gel packs are those little traveling packets you get from time to time. These little buggers work to dry things out after you accidentally get them wet. Simply place the silica gel packets all around the item you wish to dry out—like your toilet phone—and wait for a few hours.

48.
Drip a few essential oil drops on your toilet paper roll.

Your bathroom can be a pretty stinky place. If you want to make it a little easier to stand, simply drip a few of your favorite essential oil drops to the toilet paper roll on the inside of your toilet paper. That way, every time you roll the toilet paper out, you can spread a few layers of freshness throughout your bathroom. This is the easiest way to bring good-smelling vibes into your bathroom.

49.
Place old newspaper at the bottom of your garbage bag.

I hate garbage juice. Garbage juice that leaks out of your garbage bag when you take out the garbage is literally one of the worst things in the world. If you want to remove this madness-creating element from your life, you can easily maneuver this DIY technique. Simply crumple up some newspapers and place them at the bottom of your brand new garbage bag. This provides an additional layer against grime and gook and further helps to absorb all gross odors.

50.
Clean up your blender with this essential hack.

If you're often mixing up delicious smoothies and snacks in your blender, you HAVE to use this hack to make cleanup easier. After you've created your daily smoothie, simply fill the blender up with warm water. Add about a tablespoon of dish soap. Afterwards, allow the mixture to blend for about 30 seconds. This soap gets to every single section of your blender. Rinse out your blender and let it dry.

51.
Get fabric "balls" off your clothes and freshen your look with this hack.

Do you ever get those annoying fabric balls on your nice pieces of clothing? If the answer is yes, your clothes are "pilling." You can easily rid your clothes of pills with this awesome hack. Simply shave off the small pills with a razor. Make sure that these razors you use for this hack are super-dull so that you won't cut your clothes.

Chapter 4: DIY Beauty Hacks

Women all over the world have to work incredibly hard to look beautiful—and then they step out of their houses looking flawless and perfect. If you want to maximize your time, your money, and your exterior beauty, you should look to these really unique beauty hacks. Everything is covered: your lips, your hair, your concealer, your nails—everything!

1.
Get your lipstick off your teeth.

The old lipstick on the teeth problem is seemingly never-ending. However, if you utilize this awesome hack, you can avoid this problem with beautiful ease. After you apply your lipstick, stick your finger in your mouth, starting on the left side. Touch your teeth and then pull your finger out, making that very childlike "popping" noise of days past. Do this for every area of your teeth to remove the excess lipstick from the area of your lips.

2.
Utilize white eye shadow to make your eyes pop.

When you want your eyes to pop, you might look to white eye shadow. All you have to do is place a single layer of white eye shadow on your eyelid. After that, add whatever color you want on top. The white works to keep the other colors from rubbing off throughout the day, as well. Furthermore, you can add more white eye shadow up by your eyebrows to enhance the color.

3.
Look to mascara for eyeliner.

This doesn't seem to make sense, does it? After all: you have eyeliner for one thing and mascara for another. However, if you're in a hurry or don't want to buy two things, you can just position a small eyeliner brush over your mascara wand and line your eyes with the liquid. This is a super hack that helps you get your eyes lined very quickly.

4.
Having trouble applying concealer beneath your eyes? Try this unique hack.

When you apply your facial concealer properly, you can completely cover up the crazy bags and circles beneath your eyes. Do this by creating a triangle out of the concealer. Simply dot the concealer beneath your eyes and then create "triangles" beneath your eyes. This completely covers up your eye circles.

5.
Make your regular eyeliner "liquid" in 15 seconds!

If you want the smoldering temptress look of liquid eyeliner but want to stick with your super-cheap drugstore eyeliner, try out this really cool hack. Simply take your regular drugstore eyeliner and light a flame directly over the eyeliner for one second. Allow the eyeliner to cool for 15 seconds before applying it to your eyes and delivering this intense gaze.

6.
Create a beautiful DIY manicure.

Graduated manicures involve the gradation from color to color to create a beautiful sunset-like creation on your nails. They're super easy to do if you utilize makeup sponges. Begin by painting the colors you want ON the sponge. Next, press the sponge directly to your nail. Do this over and over again, always painting in the same spot to create the same pattern. This way: each of your nails looks exactly the same!

7.
Apply baby powder to your lashes for stunning lash power.

You don't need an eyelash curler or any false lashes to magnify your lashes. Instead, you can apply baby powder to your lashes with a cotton swab. Run the powder over your lashes AFTER the mascara application. Next, apply another layer of mascara to ultimately beautify your lashes.

8.
Make an X in the center of your top lip to apply proper lip liner.

If you don't know how to apply your lip liner, you can utilize this awesome hack! Simply create an X in the center of your top lip. This X will join up with the two upper points of your lips. From there, you can begin your lines. This gears the rest of your lines to match up appropriately. After you fill the lines in, you can apply lipstick for super-full lips.

9.
Remove split ends.

Don't go to your stylist to take care of your split ends all the time. Instead, twist your hair at the bottom and snip the "outside" of the hair to remove all the split ends you see poking out from the spiral. This way, your hair will look very shiny and beautiful—without the need to shell out money at the stylist.

10.
Quickly style your hair with a topknot.

If you need a super-stylish get-up in an instant, utilize this hack. Simply create a high ponytail at the top of your head and secure it. Next, divide this ponytail into two portions. Twist these two sections up in opposite directions, and secure them on top of your head to create a perfect topknot.

11.
Create your own DIY dry shampoo.

It's happened to all of us: we've woken up late, don't have enough time to shower, and therefore must go to work—without clean hair? However, this marvelous dry shampoo hack allows us to clean our hair without taking a shower. Simply mix together ⅓ cup cornstarch and 8 drops lavender essential oil. Apply the created mix to the roots of your hair and then comb the dry shampoo. This relieves your hair of oil and allows it to smell fresh and clean.

12.
Get perfect winged eyeliner.

If you want to have winged eyeliner—and you want that winged eyeliner to look perfect—simply look to this awesome hack. First, draw the wing at the outside of your eye, exactly where you want it. Note that you should start small and then make it bigger as you go. After you draw the wing, you can fade in the rest of your eyeliner for the other parts of your eye.

13.
Fix up your French manicure with a rubber band.

When your fingernail chips at the end of your French manicure, you can easily fix it with this rubber band hack. Simply place your rubber band over your nail, directly at the edge of your white polish. Next, apply brand-new polish in the area that's chipped, and allow it to dry. This way, you won't have to completely redo the entire thing.

14.
Place a business card above your lashes for perfect eyelash mascara application.

If you want to make your eyelashes super-full, use this awesome hack. Simply place your business card at the top of your eyelashes. Next, apply the mascara up on your lashes, not being worried about how high you apply the mascara because you won't "get" your skin. Remember that you can't use this business card for anything else!

15.
Create awesome nail art with a Band-Aid.

The sticky part of your Band-Aid comes with a complete DIY nail hack. The edge of your Band-Aid probably has tiny "holes" that allow your skin to breathe when you use it. If you place this part over your already painted (and dried) nail, you can make "polka dots" over the color with a different color. Pretty neat, huh?

16.
Always check your makeup in the natural light of your car.

When you do your makeup in the morning, you probably only look at yourself in the safety of your bathroom. However, if you want to be safe, you should always check your makeup in your car, in the natural light, before you head into public. That way, you'll see how your makeup looks in the natural light and you'll note if you should alter your makeup blendings or colors.

17.
Always have one makeup brush for applying and one for blending.

So: when you're blending and applying your various colors, it's essential that you keep some things separate so that your makeup doesn't become muddy on your face. If you apply one chosen color to your eyes with one brush, you should always blend that color with a different brush. Keep your colors and your blenders separate—always!

18.
Remove glitter nail polish with Elmer's Glue.

Thank goodness for Elmer's! When you hate the glitter nail polish removal process (which we all do), you should look to Elmer's Glue. Begin by utilizing glue actually ON your nail BEFORE you paint on the glitter nail polish. This allows you to peel your glitter nail polish off all at once rather than allowing it to chip away piece after piece.

19.
Create a manicure with Elmer's Glue, as well.

Back to Elmer's for more beauty hacks. If you utilize Elmer's Glue in the area around your nails (on your skin, I mean), you won't have to worry about painting your skin and then having a messy manicure. Instead, your glue will just peel off with all the "mess-ups" along the way, revealing a perfect manicure.

20.
Utilize eye shadow on your lips for the perfect, full lip color.

If you want to make your lips really POP, you have to utilize eye shadow. Simply apply your regular lipstick or color to your lips. Next, utilize a same-colored frosted eye shadow on top of the lips to make them really pop. Remember that frosted eye shadow is thicker than regular eye shadow. Therefore, it really is the essential element of this hack.

21.
Flat iron your braids for awesome waves.

Remember how much you love the waves you get after you braid your hair? Well. You can make those waves last longer with this hack. Simply braid your entire head and then flat iron each of these braids. Allow them to cool. Afterwards, loosen your braids and check out your long-lasting waves!

22.
Bring light into the dark corners of your eyes.

When you look to lighter-colored eye shadows for the smaller, inside corners of your eyes, you can really make your eyes POP and look younger. This light, brighter color can remove the regular darkness that occurs in this area. Work to simply apply a small, lightly brushed color of this shadow into this area. Enjoy the results!

23.
Apply perfume like a pro.

Perfume doesn't last the entire day if you don't apply it to your body correctly. If you want your perfume to last you all day, you have to hit yourself in the right areas. Simply do this by applying your perfume behind your ears, at your throat, behind your knee, and on the inside of your wrist.

24.
Make your nail polish set more quickly.

If you want your nail polish to dry and set super quickly, you can try out this essential hack. Simply prepare a bowl of ice water. After you paint your nails, dip your nails into the ice water for five seconds. This helps to immediately set the polish and help your nails stay radiant.

25.
Put mouthwash on your bruises.

If you're a bit clumsy (aren't we all?) you might want to look into this hack to remove the sign of bruises from your body. If you apply mouthwash to the bruise on your body, you can help the bruise look instantly better. Furthermore, the bruise will feel better, giving you instant relief.

26.
DIY bronzer with at-home ingredients.

Even if you hate the sun or have very sensitive skin, you can look like you spend every day at the beach with this awesome DIY hack. Simply mix together 1 tsp. cocoa, 1 tsp. cinnamon, 2 tsp. cornstarch, and 1 tsp. nutmeg. You can add it to your face with your regular makeup brush and look remarkable. Furthermore, this brings a holiday scent to your face that will be scrumptious during the holiday months!

27.
Remove makeup from your shirt collars with this essential hack.

Makeup on the shirt collar again? Not to worry with this awesome hack. You can simply position a bit of shaving cream over the stain and then wipe the makeup and the shaving cream off the collar with a slightly wet cloth. The shaving cream doesn't alter your clothes at all. Furthermore, you won't even have to change your clothes!

28.
Make your pimples slightly less visible with Visine.

Visine, the de-red eye solution, helps to make your pimples decrease in size. Simply put the Visine on your pimples and allow it to sit for about five minutes. After a few hours, the redness will fade and your zit can be easily covered up with concealer.

29.
DIY your own lip stain.

If you want to try a different lip stain, why not try to utilize some Kool-Aid? Simply stain your lips with the actual powder. The powder lasts on your lips actually all day rather than coming off by lunch. Remember that this is the most inexpensive way to try a variety of interesting colors!

30.
Create a leave-in conditioner.

If your hair is apt to tangle throughout the day, you should definitely look to this awesome DIY leave-in conditioner hack to make your life easier. Simply bring one part conditioner to three parts water into a spray bottle and spray your hair throughout the day to keep your hair from tangling with itself. Works like a charm!

31.
Create a "long" ponytail with short hair.

If you want to create a long ponytail for a long, luxurious "mane," try this awesome hack. Simply divide your hair horizontally around the area of your ear. Next, pull the top portion of your hair into a high ponytail. Pull the bottom half of your ponytail into a lower ponytail. The top ponytail will conceal the bottom ponytail, but the hair will come together in a unique way to make a "long" ponytail.

32.
Use hand cream to smooth frizzing hair.

If you're without any leave-in conditioner but you DO have hand cream (because who doesn't have hand cream?) you can look to this awesome hack. When your hair starts to frizz, simply glide hand cream over your hair after first applying the stuff to your hands, so it isn't too thick on your hair strands.

33.
Run a dryer sheet through staticky hair.

If your hair is often static-ridden and all over the place, you can use a handy-dandy dryer sheet to keep things under control. Simply run it through your hair when you see that your hair is becoming staticky. Furthermore, this will allow your hair to smell AWESOME throughout the day.

34.
Remove all makeup with coconut oil.

Super-healthy coconut oil offers many anti-aging benefits for your skin. What's more? Coconut oil is absolutely perfect for removing makeup from your face. Place a bit of coconut oil on a pad and work to remove your makeup with the pad. The coconut oil soaks up the oil of the makeup easily.

35.
Make a baking soda at-home mask to remove blackheads.

Any time you're experiencing a breakout, you should look to this essential DIY mask. Simply mix together baking soda and water—just enough water to create a paste. Next, put the paste on your face and allow it to dry. Remove the mask with a washcloth and completely moisturize your face immediately.

36.
Treat your cuticles with lip gloss.

When your cuticles look a little drab, a little less-than, you can look to lip gloss to brighten them up. Cuticle treatment is an all-extensive, expensive maneuver. However, you can utilize lip gloss from the dollar store for this easy hack. Just apply the lip gloss to your cuticles and allow them to sit for a vibrant shine.

37.
Use conditioner for shaving cream.

When you travel everywhere, you won't want to bring both shaving cream AND conditioner, will you? I didn't think so. If you simply utilize conditioner for your shaving cream, you can completely remove your hairs safely and with moisturizing benefits, without bringing along both containers.

38.
Place deodorant on the inside of your thighs to keep from chafing.

During the summer, everyone suffers from chafing. Luckily, if you utilize this awesome beauty hack, you'll have a seamless summer. Simply slide deodorant over the insides of your thighs and live a life of freedom! Keep reapplying when you begin to sweat.

39.
Skip over the eyeliner step with this awesome beauty hack.

If you don't have time to apply eyeliner—and who does in this crazy day-and-age of continuous preparation and going out and coming in?—you should utilize this awesome hack. Simply apply your mascara like you normally do. Then, when you get to the very root of your eyelashes, you can wiggle the mascara brush ever so slightly. This allows the darkness to ramp up onto your skin, giving you a smoky look.

40.
Avoid people noticing your chipping manicure with this unique hack.

When your manicure begins to chip, it can be pretty heartbreaking. If you utilize this awesome hack, however, you can completely eliminate embarrassment. Simply paint a layer of glitter nail polish over your nails in order to distract other people's eyes from your imperfections. This allows you to go quite a while between manicures!

41.
Utilize lipstick for blush when you're on-the-go.

More women take lipstick with them on their way to and from events. However, many less women take blush with them. If you want to look fresh and vibrant on your way to your next event—but you can't take everything along with you—simply utilize some lipstick as a cream blush to brighten your face. Remember to tap lightly to add this extra layer of brightness.

42.
Combine highlighter with your body lotion.

If you want your legs to look long and gleaming, utilize this awesome mid-summer hack. Simply mix together highlighter with some body lotion and rub it all over your body. Make sure to have a mixture of about 2 parts body lotion with 1 part highlighter. Apply as you need to!

43.
Look to clear mascara to seal your black lashes.

If you don't like utilizing waterproof mascara but you still want your black lashes to look fresh and clean all day long, look to this one useful hack. Simply swipe black mascara over your top lashes and then cover the black lashes with clear mascara. This allows your mascara to stay perfect on your lashes without smearing throughout the day.

44.
Use a credit card to maximize your "cat eye" look.

If you want to make a perfect line angled out from your eye for a groovy "cat eye" look—but you have trouble making a straight line—you can look to this unique hack. Simply angle your credit card out from your eye in the exact angle you require. Next, powder the area around your eye and to your credit card to create your look.

45.
Look to peppermint oil to boost your lip look.

Are you looking for an extra boost for your lips? Peppermint essential oil works to plump up your lips and make you look really youthful and sexy. Simply dab peppermint oil over your lips and then rub your lips together like you would a regular lip gloss. Furthermore, peppermint has anti-hunger properties, keeping you away from the snacks!

46.
Curl your eyelashes and apply your eyeliner at the same time.

This unique hack allows you to line your eyes and curl your eyelashes at the same time when you're in a rush. (And who likes to work on their makeup all day long? Not me.) Simply line the bottom edge of the top portion of your eyelash curler with eyeliner. Next, curl your eyelashes, making sure that the part you've lined with eyeliner meets up with the line of your eye. Next: reveal your stunning, super-easy look.

47.
Utilize white eyeliner to hide a hangover.

If you're feeling really, really tired or hung over, look to this unique hack to make your eyes pop and make yourself look AWAKE. After all: as long as you tell yourself you're awake and feeling good, you'll feel like you are—right? Simply line your eyes with light or white eyeliner to allow your eyes to pop. Note that you should do this especially on the bottom line of your eye.

48.
Lighten foundation with white moisturizer.

It's easy to purchase foundation that's too dark for you—especially if you're in the wake of losing your summer tan. If you don't want to buy a brand-new bottle of foundation and simply need to lighten the foundation a few shades, utilize this awesome hack. Simply mix together a bit of white face moisturizer with your foundation. Do this just a bit at a time until you get your desired color.

49.
Warm up your mascara before applying it with this unique hack.

Your mascara needs a few moments to warm up before you apply it. Do this by sticking your entire mascara tube into your bra as you get ready in the morning. Then: remove your mascara tube and realize the magic of warmed-up mascara. It glides onto your lashes so much easier!

50.
Place Vaseline on your wrists or neck before you apply perfume.

If you want to make your perfume last all day long, look to this unique hack. Simply rub Vaseline over your pressure points—the places you generally utilize perfume. Then, spray your perfume as you normally do. The Vaseline brings the perfume into itself, allowing it to stay on your body all day long.

51.
Spread a bit of white makeup pencil to the center of your lip to bring layered shine.

If your lips need a boost to make them look fuller, utilize this awesome hack. Simply spread a bit of white eye pencil in the center of both of your lips. Next, apply lip gloss over the pencil, spreading it well to make it look extra full and extra glossy.

52.
Focus on only one element of your face when you're limited on time.

Okay: so—sometimes you wake up late, right? And then you have a very limited amount of time in front of the mirror. When you have this limited amount of time, you should look to focus only on one very essential part of your face: your eyes or your mouth. Play up your eyes OR play up your lips. Don't focus on both—you won't have time, and they'll both look half-done.

53.
Add contact solution to your clumpy mascara.

Mascara clumps pretty easily, becoming terribly annoying during your morning routine. If you want to de-clump it a little bit and make it last for you a little longer, you can drip a few drops of contact solution into the tube. Shake the closed tube around with the solution in, and add a few more to get your desired consistency. You just need to liven it up a little bit!

54.
Keep a few face wipes by your bed if you don't want to wash your face every night.

Ugh. The nightly ritual gets a little annoying sometimes, doesn't it? Every time you lie down in your bed and realize you forgot to wash your face, the utter realization that you'll have a zit in the morning really kills you. However, if you just keep a few face wipes by the bed every night, you can simply reach over, wipe your face, and fall asleep. Phew.

55.
Sleep with two pillows—not one—to reduce puffy eyes.

When you sleep appropriately, you can look less tired. Simply prop yourself up on two pillows to allow your face to drain all of its fluid. This allows you to wake up looking stunning, fresh, and ready to conquer the day!

56.
Make your lipstick "matte" without buying matte lipstick.

If you want to give your lipstick a new look—without buying new lipstick—check out this unique hack. The matte look is very in right now. In order to achieve it, you simply have to dab concealer over your lips before applying the gloss over the concealer. This gives your gloss a completely different look.

57.
Heal your feet while you sleep.

If your feet are tired, cracked, and sore, you can look to this hack to make your feet look young and fresh again. Simply apply Vaseline or moisturizer to your feet and then put socks over your feet. Sleep overnight and then wake up to your brand-new feet!

58.
Make your smile brighter by brushing with baking soda.

If your teeth just aren't up to snuff right now, you can look to this unique hack. Simply begin to brush your teeth with baking soda, three times a day. Baking soda brightens your teeth on a maximum level. Furthermore, it works to alleviate bad breath and fight disease. You don't even have to use toothpaste anymore!

59.
Halt runs in your tights with hairspray.

How often has your outfit been ruined just because your tights have a run in them? All the time, right? Well: if you utilize this unique hack (taught to me by the mother of DIY, my grandmother), you can stop runs in their tracks. Simply spray the runs with hairspray, and go on your way.

60.
Get rid of stretch marks with baby oil.

Stretch marks after babies or after losing weight can be a real bore. If you want to cleanse your skin and make it look vibrant and new again, you should look to baby oil. Simply rub it on your body every morning, noon, and night going forward, and then watch as your stretch marks disappear!

61.
Make your hair look full with a bit of eye shadow.

If your hair is a little weak in places—a little thin—you can maximize the appearance of volume with this awesome hack. Using dark eye shadow, simply brush a bit of the color into your part. This allows your hair to look extra thick!

62.
Eliminate your up-do flyaways with this awesome hack.

Every time you put your hair in an up-do, you have to deal with all the flyaway problems along the way. To completely remove those flyaways, you can just spray some hairspray on an old toothbrush and then brush at the flyaways on your head to keep them down.

63.
Keep your bobby pins in place with hairspray.

How often throughout the day do you have to alter the location of your bobby pins? All the time, right? Well: if you want to halt that business, you can simply spray your bobby pins with hairspray and then pop them into your hair. This allows them to stay in place all day long—keeping your hair in place, as well.

64.
T-shirts are better at drying your hair than towels.

This might seem like a stretch, but bear with me. Every time you try to dry your hair with a towel, the towel becomes damp incredibly fast and your hair—is still super-duper wet. If you want to avoid this, simply utilize a T-shirt to wrap around your head. This absorbs the water instantly and helps you stay warm and dry.

65.
Wash your roots in the sink.

If you're running late and you don't have any dry shampoo on hand, you can just wash your roots in the sink with your regular shampoo. Make sure not to get any of the rest of your hair wet. After all: the roots are the dust and grime-collecting areas of your body. If you only wash your roots, your hair will dry out super-fast on your way to work!

Chapter 5: Fitness and Exercise Hacks

Weight loss and exercise are two pretty essential elements of our lives, leaving us with better health and thinner waistlines. However! It can be difficult to force ourselves into weight loss action. Look to these remarkable techniques in order to lose weight the easy way and age gracefully throughout the years.

1.
Listen to your favorite podcast ONLY when you exercise.

We all have our favorite podcasts, right? They're a pleasure to listen to. Now: what if you told yourself you were only allowed to listen to your favorite podcast when you were exercising? Don't allow yourself to listen to it when you're sitting down. Pretty soon: you'll start feeling guilty when you are listening to your favorite podcast and NOT exercising.

2.
Try the above with your favorite audio book.

Try listening to a book you're really interested in while you're exercising—and only allow yourself to listen to the audio book when you're exercising. This way: you will want to get back on the "horse," so to speak, in order to listen to the next chapter! Make it a game for yourself.

3.
Buy good-looking workout clothes.

When you wear old pajamas to exercise, you won't feel too amped up next time you step out the door to go jogging. However, if you buy proper exercise clothes and feel like you "look" the part, you'll ultimately feel awesome. You'll feel like you're on top of the world. And you'll become addicted to the feeling!

4.
Download an app like jog.fm.

Jog.fm plays all the music you already have on your phone but makes sure to match your pace while you run. Therefore, it analyzes how fast you're running, analyzes your music, and gives you the appropriate songs to rev your engine.

5.
Create an exercise schedule and make sure to stick to it.

If you create a schedule for yourself even a month ahead of time, you'll feel resigned to it. You'll feel like you have committed yourself to something rather than always asking yourself: should I exercise today? Do I want to? You'll know when your rest days are and when your work out days are. And you'll see results.

6.
Run one minute per day and add an additional minute every day.

If you've never run before in your life, try out this unique hack to build endurance. Simply run for one minute per day—adding an additional minute each day. Therefore, you run one minute the first day, two minutes the second day, and three minutes the third day. This will fuel you with motivation to run 30 minutes after 30 days.

7.
Run with a partner and talk the whole time.

If you talk and run, you'll build your endurance as you go. This means that you're forcing your breath to regulate. Furthermore, it shows that you're not overdoing it, and it keeps your mind far away from the pain your feet and knees might be experiencing—especially on long runs.

8.
Create an "exercise" game during your favorite television show.

Remember drinking games? Drink every time the person says "whatever," or drink every time someone curses? Utilize this awesome hack to get yourself to exercise in much the same way. Every time a character does something he or she "does" often, you have to do 20 lunges or 10 pushups. This will get your heart revving during your regular programs.

9.
Create an exercise playlist with the exact amount of exercise time you want.

Rather than setting a specific time on your watch, why not judge the amount of time you've exercised with this unique hack? Simply create a playlist with the exact amount of time on it—say 30 or 45 minutes—you wish to exercise. That way: time will simply accelerate as you listen to your favorite tunes!

10.
Keep some gym clothes and shoes with you at all times.

If you simply have your gym clothes and shoes with you in your car at all times, you'll have the ability to exercise wherever and whenever you please. Even if you weren't planning on exercising initially, you can hit the pavement when the mood strikes you. You have to go where the mood takes you, right?

11.
Sleep in your exercise clothes for early-morning workouts.

If you want to wake up and exercise but find it hard to get up in the morning, simply wear your exercise clothes to bed and then wake up in them, ready to exercise! This way: you are already ready to go, ready to hit it, without wasting time.

12.
Place frozen fruit in your regular water bottle.

Frozen fruit brightens your normal water bottle with a bit of added flavor. Furthermore, it keeps your water extra cold and delicious. Drink all your water to get a tasty treat at the bottom—the perfect post-workout treat!

13.
Wrap plastic wrap around your touchscreen phone if it's about to rain on your run.

If you're worried it's going to rain on your run, you can still go running AND tote your iPhone. Do this by wrapping your phone in plastic wrap. This allows your phone to be protected from the rain. Furthermore, it allows you to still do your touchscreen functions—through the plastic! What a great hack.

14.
Find a mid-television exercise you could do.

If you hate going to the gym but want to get your heart rate pumping while you watch television after work, look to these awesome exercises: running in place, jumping rope, or hula-hooping. If you work to do something, you can maximize your time in front of the television and wait for the weekend for more vibrant exercises.

15.
Cycle on the exercise bike and play video games on your television.

When you sit on the exercise bike, you can still exercise your mind with this super-fun hack. Cycle as quickly as you can and then play your video games at the same time. As the game intensifies, your feet will begin to pedal faster and faster, making your heart rate quicken. You start to feel like you're actually in the game!

16.
Always make yourself "work" for your snacks.

Before taking a snack from the kitchen, tell yourself you always have to exercise with pushups or sit-ups. Remind yourself that every lit bit "counts" in the long run: whether that means a few extra snacks contribute to weight gain or a few extra pushups contribute to weight loss.

17.
Give yourself two dollars every time you exercise rather than joining a gym.

Gyms are expensive. However, if you simply exercise outside and then pay yourself the same amount of money you would have spent at the gym that day, you can really save up for something nice! Buy yourself something: new exercise clothes, a healthy snack, or even a nice vacation with the money you've saved over six months!

18.
Make your own DIY weights at home.

Joining a gym is expensive. Buying your own weights is expensive. Is there anything in the weightlifting world that isn't expensive? Well: if you utilize this unique hack, you can say hello to muscles and goodbye to expensive weightlifting. Simply utilize soup cans for weight-focused workouts for a lot of reps. If you want to enhance the weight, look to duct taping two or three cans together. Alternately, you can look to backpacks stocked with books, spare tires, or cast iron pans.

19.
Look to purchase a pedometer to enhance your step numbers.

You're always burning calories when you're moving around. If you're wearing a pedometer, you'll make moving around a sort of game for yourself—instead of a ruthless thing called exercise. Furthermore, a recent scientific study notes that 10,000 steps a day—which is really nothing—is pretty active while 12,500 steps per day is considered awesome.

20.
Watch personal trainers at the gym instead of hiring your own.

This is a little sneaky. However, next time you're at your gym, note the people with their own personal trainers and try to assess what the personal trainer is telling that person. Note which exercises they do, how many reps they do, how the trainer alters their form, etc. This way, you can apply what they're doing to your own workout.

21.
Look for steps.

Steps are built-in cardio machines all around the world. Find them to strengthen your butt, your quads, and your calves in essential ways. Furthermore, this exercise is easy on your knees and really low-impact compared to running. Head to your local park, your local stadium—really anywhere for this workout.

22.
Schedule text reminders to yourself to tell yourself to exercise.

This one's pretty sneaky. If you schedule your workouts ahead of time and then pre-send your text messages to yourself via OhDontForget.com, you can actually convince yourself—from the past—to exercise in the future. Therefore, you can never, ever forget about a plan to head to the gym again.

23.
Always go for a walk to clear your mind and de-stress yourself.

So often, people will get stressed and head to the refrigerator to calm their feelings. However, you can easily calm your cortisol (stress) hormone levels by going for a walk, instead. Furthermore, eating while you're feeling super-stressed is an incredibly bad habit, resulting in our overweight population. If you break the habit now by actually exercising instead, you're giving yourself a better chance at longevity.

24.
Always get some "fun" exercise on vacation.

What is your typical vacation? Let me guess: drinks on the beach, all day, every day. And that's fine, of course! After all: drinking in the sun is really relaxing and wonderful. However, in order to enhance your lifestyle, it's essential to get some much-needed fun exercise in your vacation schedule. Do this by: going water skiing, going snorkeling, heading out for a long exploratory hike, etc.!

25.
Try cleaning the house.

There are a TON of cleaning hacks in a previous chapter you can try out to both clean your house AND exercise. Every time you scrape at your carpet with the squeegee, you're exercising your arms. Every time you scrub at your sink and bathtub, you're breaking a sweat. If you just get into the nitty-gritty of your house, you'll also get into the nitty-gritty of your fat cells. Awesome, right? Think about 4 calories a minute.

26.
If you live in a big city, sell your car.

In bigger cities, you have the option of looking to public transportation to get around. Force yourself out of the ease of your vehicle and look to the modernity of public transportation to lose weight instantly. Your gut will seal up in a few weeks; your legs will gain muscle. And think of all the marvelous things you'll see along your walk to work!

27.
Adopt a dog.

This is a big step, sure. But research shows that getting a dog is one of the biggest steps toward greater health in the world. When you have a dog, you HAVE to go outside and have fun with him or her. You have to head out, walk around, maybe even run a little bit, in order to get your dog's energy out of his or her system. Research shows that you can lose up to 19 pounds a year!

28.
Ask for a standing desk at work.

If you want to reduce your back pain AND help yourself lose weight during the work week, you might want to opt for a standing desk. This will strengthen your back and your shoulders. Furthermore, research shows that people who sit all day, every day are 54% more likely to have a heart attack than other people.

29.
Go out dancing instead of to a pub.

If you have the choice between going out to a sit-down pub or going out dancing, you HAVE to choose dancing. Seriously. The benefits of going out dancing are unrivaled. You're getting your heart rate up, you're feeling the endorphins, and you're bonding with your friends on a whole new level! Awesome.

30.
Go to the gym when people are "away."

So: going to the gym when it's busy, when all of the exercise bikes and machines are taken, and not a single piece of equipment is dry from people's sweat, is very loathsome. However, if you head to the gym during off-hours—if possible—you'll have a much more efficient time. If you go during the middle of the day, for example, during your lunch hour—you'll hit non-busy hours AND you'll have an extra boost for your next hours at work.

31.
wear while you're exercising.
(Maybe not in public.)

This is a funny one. Research shows that people who swear when they exercise experience less pain than people who don't swear. This fuels a "fight or flight" response in your body that allows your body to push through the pain more efficiently and keep you in line with your goals. Try to whisper the words to yourself if you don't want to offend your neighbors!

32.
Always write down all of the food you eat.

If you're looking to lose weight, it's essential that you start monitoring your food intake with this hack. Write down every single thing you eat during the day. You don't have to necessarily track your calories—although apps like LoseIt! make it pretty convenient. If you want, you can monitor everything you do in this same notebook: from your exercise to your sleep hours.

33.
Skip milk and sugar and try cinnamon.

Both milk and sugar in your coffee fuel a ton of extra calories that your body doesn't need. However, if you utilize a bit of cinnamon—always at the back of the coffee shop, at that station—you can eliminate your sugar cravings, lower your bad cholesterol, and boost your brain functions.

34.
Always use a small plate rather than a dinner plate.

If you choose the smaller plate rather than the bigger plate for your meals, you can automatically reduce the amount of calories you eat. You won't be as apt to put as many items on your plate when it's a smaller plate. Studies actually show that you could decrease your caloric intake by about 20 percent!

35.
Always use fresh vegetables rather than canned vegetables.

All items in cans: whether they're beans or soups or vegetables, contain a TON of sodium. Therefore, some of these items are actually negating their former health benefits when you eat them. If you look to fresh (or frozen) items rather than canned items, you'll fuel yourself with better nutrition.

36.
Never watch television and eat at the same time.

TV dinners are over with this fitness and health hack. When you watch television and eat at the same time, your brain allows you to make some pretty poor health and food choices. Therefore, if you give your time and energy to your food—rather than to anything else—you'll give yourself the time to make correct choices moving forward.

Chapter 6: DIY Tips to Make Your Life Easier

Life is hard. The phrase is uttered by every pair of lips, all over the world. If you look to these awesome DIY hacks, you can make every minute of every day just a tad easier. You can make every minute of every day brim with earnest possibility. Hello, hope for the future!

1.
Heat up your microwavable leftovers with more efficiency.

How often does your microwaving leave you with a lackluster, cold-in-the-middle dinner? Ugh. All the time, right? If you utilize this hack, however, your meals will heat up evenly and you won't waste as much electricity and time. Simply create a "circle" in the center of the meal you're about to enjoy. Then, heat your meal however you normally would to reveal a very delicious end result.

2.
Stack all your dresser clothes in a vertical fashion.

I always lose track of old clothes because they're hiding from me, beneath all the other clothes in my dresser that I utilize all the time. This hack allows me to see everything I miss wearing all the time. I simply stack everything vertically, making sure to alternate colors to make everything pop out at me.

3.
Chew gum while you're slicing onions.

Every time I am slicing and dicing onions in the kitchen, I come out with tears streaming down my face. However, when I chew gum, the tears don't come. I don't really understand why; essentially, your "glands" are so involved with the water in your mouth that they don't think to create new tears.

4.
Create a stand for your iPhone with an old cassette case.

Those old tape cassette cases you having lying around in random places in your house can see new light with this unique hack. Simply remove the side with the "hinge" slot. Place the flat end of the tape cassette case on the table with the hinged part propped up. Slip the phone into the hinged slot and enjoy the ease with which you handle your iPhone.

5.
When you're almost finished eating your jar of Nutella with a spoon, look to this delicious hack.

When your Nutella smear—the chocolate and hazelnut delight that everyone dreams about—is getting down on its last leg, you should plop a few ice cream balls into it for enriched flavor. This provides the perfect ice cream topping and the absolute essential sugar treat for your next movie night.

6.
Make sure you drink enough water with this hack.

You have to drink enough water. Research blares the information at us. We are over 60% water, ourselves, and therefore water is the best thing to drink to keep our minds awake and our bodies energized. Take your regular water bottle and mark throughout the day how much water you should have drank by then. For example, you should drink at least two inches down by 8 a.m., four inches down by 10 a.m., etc. Do this every day to keep your intake up.

7.
Iron your collar with your hair straightener.

Maybe you don't straighten your hair anymore because you're going the "natural" route. Regardless, you still need to keep that hair straightener around for the future. You can iron your collar—that ratty thing you need to spiff up every now and again—with the straightener by placing it on medium and ironing over it to make it flat. Seriously. It works!

8.
Bring your bagel to work in a container you already have.

Remember those old CD spindles? You can re-use those things with this hack. Keep your bagel fresh on your way to work by sticking the bagel inside the CD spindle and then positioning the plastic container overtop. This way: your bagel stays safe on your commute and you can eat it whenever you please!

9.
Create pancake mix ahead of time and pour it into a ketchup bottle.

If you want to keep your house very clean without any messes AND you want pancakes all the time, you need to look at this hack. Create a bunch of pancake mix and then pour the pancake mix into an empty ketchup bottle. Squirt the pancake mix out onto the skillet when you want to make pancakes and allow it to chill all the other times. See? No mess!

10.
Sick of having friends borrow things and never return them?

Your friends are envious of all the cool things you own. Who wouldn't be? However, when they ask to borrow things, it's essential that they return them. You're not a donation service! Anyway: in order to remember who has what, you can start taking pictures of them with the things they borrowed. Keep them on your phone to remember in the future.

11.
Serve condiments in a muffin tin at large outdoor parties.

Muffin tins become your ultimate lifesaver at outdoor parties and BBQs. When you need to tote around a plethora of condiments for burgers, for example, you can simply position your mustard, your ketchup, your onions—everything—in the muffin tin for people to serve themselves as they please. Super easy and fun!

12.
Slice cakes and cheeses perfectly with dental floss.

Do you have trouble making perfect slices in your cakes and cheeses? If so, you should definitely use this unique hack. Simply rip off a long piece of dental floss and slice the floss through your cake. Do this all throughout the cake to make perfect slices. It takes the hassle out of "slicing," doesn't it?

13.
Tab your straw to keep it in place.

It's really smart to drink canned Cokes and other soft drinks out of a straw. After all: that saves you teeth all the hardship of coloring and all that. However, it's frustrating when your straw rises out of the can and falls to the ground! If you want to keep it in place, simply slip your straw through the tab on the can. That way: it stays in place, ready for you to drink from it any time you want.

14.
Bake tortillas in upside-down muffin pans.

When you flip your muffin tins upside down, another whole world is created! Simply position your tortillas in those "in-between" areas and allow them to bake at 375 degrees Fahrenheit for 10 minutes. This gives them a serious crunch for Taco Bell-like crunchy tacos.

15.
Always position a square of cardboard in your plastic bags.

Why would you do this, you ask? Well: when you utilize a plastic bag to transport documents, it's hard to keep them slick and straight, isn't it? If you want to protect them, you can keep that sliver of cardboard in the plastic bag at all times to give your documents something to rail up against.

16.
Light candles with a stick of spaghetti.

When you want to light candles—on a birthday cake or just for decoration—it's so incredibly easy to burn yourself. In order to light candles safely, simply light the end of a spaghetti stick and light the candles with the end. It's the perfect way to keep yourself from harm! Plus, you have plenty of spaghetti noodles lying around, I'm sure.

17.
Freeze your sponges to make ice packs.

If you're experiencing muscle pain that requires the utilization of ice packs—or if you have kids that fall down a lot—you should look into this unique hack. Simply place a normal, completely saturated sponge in a zip-lock bag and place the bag in the freezer. Allow the sponge to completely freeze. Then, when you need it, you can place the ice pack on your aches and pains. The ice pack will melt on the inside of the bag—and not all over you!

18.
Use bread tabs to label your cords.

Those cords in the back of the TV can be pretty complicated. Which cord goes to which unit? It's always hard to say. However, if you use this unique hack, you can completely eliminate confusion.

Simply label the cords on the bread tabs that come with your loaves of bread and place the tabs on the wires. This is super-clean and easy to create.

19.
Make "bacon" pancakes.

Bacon pancakes deliver all the joys of breakfast in one satisfying package. Simply begin by mixing your pancake batter and setting to the side. Then, start sizzling your bacon on the griddle. When the bacon is nearly finished cooking, pour the batter directly over the bacon, allow the batter to solidify, and then flip to cook the other half. Enjoy!

20.
Use a nice pool noodle to make your beer cooler float.

Yes, yes. You can truly use your cooler while you're in the middle of the pool, sunning. Simply slice old pool noodles to fit the sides of your cooler. Then, pull a rope through the center of the pool noodles to create a "circle" around the cooler. Make sure to do all you can to keep the cooler tight in the pool noodles, and stock your cooler with whatever you want in the water!

21.
Keep your stuff safe at the beach with this all-too-clever hack.

When you run out of tanning lotion, don't throw the bottle away! Instead, completely clean out the lotion bottle and make it into a large container. (You might have to cut off the top. Next, place your keys, money, and phone in the container to keep it safe at the beach: safe from people, safe from sand, and safe from the sun!

365 Days of DIY

22.
Find lost, tiny items by placing an old stocking over your vacuum cleaner tube.

If you just can't find the earring you lost in the dark carpet, you can look to this unique hack to truly get your things back. Simply position an old stocking over the vacuum tube and keep it there with a rubber band. Next, roam your carpet with the tube to pull up things. Dirt will go through the stocking, but things like earrings won't!

23.
Keep your pot from boiling over with this unique hack.

When your pot begins to boil over when you're cooking—but you have a million other things to deal with at the same time—look to this awesome hack. Simply place a wooden spoon over the boiling water. The spoon will keep the water at bay, beneath it, for as long as you need! Furthermore, the spoon is there for you when you have time to stir, giving you even more extra time to do everything else!

24.
Hold cookbooks up high with a pants hanger.

You know those old pants hangers you get from retail stores with the two clips, one at each end? You can use those for this really, really important hack. When you get tired of looking over and over at the cookbook for the next instructions, you can hang your cookbook up at eye-level with these pants' hangers. Simply clip both sides of the cookbook and hang the cookbook from your cabinet. Perfect!

25.
Make your bottles ice-cold instantly.

If you bring a bottle of something back with you from the cold and you want it to be ice-cold instantly, utilize this awesome hack. Simply wrap a paper towel around the bottle. Place the bottle in the freezer for 15 minutes. After 15 minutes, the bottle will be completely ice-cold and perfect to drink!

26.
Make hanging pictures easy today!

Whenever you need to hang a picture or a frame with exact holes in the back, knowing where to put the nails in the wall can be a very serious pain. If you utilize this awesome hack, however, you can really revamp your ability to hang items. Simply photocopy the back of the frame by placing the back actually in a copier. The shadows will appear exactly where you're meant to put the holes!

27.
Create your own ice packs at home!

When you want to make your own ice packs for post-exercise or post-surgery utilization, you don't have to look to super-expensive items at the grocery store. Instead, if you bring together 3 parts water to 1 part rubbing alcohol in a zip-lock bag, the water will get really, really cold in the freezer. It will not, however, completely harden. Therefore, when you take the zip-lock bag out of the freezer, you can easily manipulate it!

28.
Dry your wet shoes in the dryer with this unique hack.

Every time you want to dry out your wet shoes, people warn you that you'll ultimately ruin your dryer OR that it'll be so noisy you'll never get any work done! However, this hack is perfect. Simply tie the shoelaces of your tennis shoes with a double knot. Bring the knot outside of the door and place the tennis shoes inside the dryer. Close the door on the knot, making sure that the knot is secure. And then: run your dryer. This keeps your tennis shoes in place!

29.
Create a watering can from an old milk carton.

Recycle old milk cartons with this unique trick. Simply clean out your old milk carton—including the cap. Next, poke about 15 tiny holes in the top of the cap. Fill the carton with water and then water your plants, allowing the water to retreat from the cap. This way, you don't need to invest in a regular watering can!

Chapter 7: DIY Recipes and Cooking Hacks

Are you a master of your kitchen, or do you find that most of the things you make in your kitchen are messy, lacking in flavor, and unfortunately inedible? If you need a little help making dinnertime the BEST time, look to the following cooking hacks for assistance. Maximize the deliciousness of your life!

1.
Cut corn off the cob with this super-easy hack.

It can be really difficult to remove the corn from the cob during a cooking session. In order to do this really easily, simply place a large ball of paper towel inside of a small bowl. Next, place the small bowl upside down inside of a larger bowl. The paper towel will keep it from slipping. Next, slice the corn off the cob vertically on top of the small bowl.

2.
Core iceberg lettuce instantly.

If you want to remove the core of your lettuce head in an instant, use this awesome hack. Simply slam the lettuce head down on your cutting board—hard. When it lands on the core, the core will simply fall out of the vegetable. Awesome!

3.
Cook pasta in about one minute.

Don't have much time to cook dinner? Many people don't know this unique hack—and it changes everything. Place all of your pasta noodles in a zip-lock bag with enough water to cover the noodles for about 10 minutes. Now the pasta will cook in about one minute. Amazing. You won't have to be over a hot stove for long!

4.
Pit an avocado with a knife.

If you find it difficult to get the pit out of the avocado because it's usually slippery and hard to grab, try this awesome hack. Simply stab the avocado pit with your sharp knife and twist the avocado pit out of the avocado with force. Make sure to do this carefully! You don't want to cut yourself.

5.
Create neat avocado cubes while the avocado is in the skin.

While the avocado still exists in its skin, it's the easiest to handle. Hold one half up, revealing the skin, and slice and dice it in neat checkerboards to create small avocado squares. Then, you can scoop them out easily with your spoon.

6.
Eat a kiwi straight from the skin.

Kiwis are prepackaged and ready for you to eat! Do this by simply slicing the very top "nub" from the kiwi. Next, take a small spoon and simply dip into the meat like it's ice cream. Eat the kiwi as you like, allowing the skin to keep all the juices packaged nicely on the inside, and then toss the kiwi skin out.

7.
Alternately, peel the kiwi with the spoon from the inside out.

Slice both of the ends off the kiwi and simply twist your spoon edge around the inside of the kiwi, taking the meat off the skin. This allows the skin to come off super-easily, without any hassle with knives.

8.
Keep your cutting board still while you're cutting on it.

Does your cutting board often roll this way and that, putting you in harm's way? If you need to keep that thing in place, you should place a towel beneath the cutting board. The towel keeps the cutting board exactly where you want it, even when you exert force.

9.
Stop allowing your butter to "thaw" before cutting it with this baking trick.

It's so annoying when you have to wait for your butter to sort of "loosen" up before you can cut it into the flour mixture when you're making biscuits or pancakes. However, if you actually grate the butter with a cheese grater, you can make it the exact consistency you require in a flash. It's so simple, I can't believe I've never thought of it before.

10.
Slice all your cherry tomatoes or grapes all at once.

It takes a long, long time to slice all the tomatoes and grapes one by one. However, if you simply place all of the cherry tomatoes together on a clear plastic lid and then place another plastic lid—of the same size—overtop, you can completely skip those steps. Do this, and then glide a knife carefully between the two lids.

11.
Add baking soda to caramelize your onions FAST.

If you want to caramelize onions but don't have the many, many minutes it requires to completely caramelize them, you can dash in about a teaspoon of baking soda while they're cooking. Science is real, and it's here to help your DIY!

12.
De-husk your corn FAST.

It can take a long time to de-husk an ear of corn. However, if you want to make things move a little more quickly, you can simply place your ear of corn in the microwave for about 15 seconds. When you remove the corn, the corn will simply slide right out of the husk. Voila!

13.
Spread nonstick spray over your cheese grater for easy grating.

No more mess when you're grating your cheese with this simple hack. Simply spray nonstick spray over your cheese grater. Next, grate your cheese and note how quick your cleanup is—while you munch on really, really delightful cheese. Yum!

14.
Get ALL the juice from lemons and limes.

It's always really difficult to get all the citrus juice from limes and lemons. However, if you first microwave them for 20 seconds, the carbohydrates in the juice will begin the breakdown process and completely liquefy when you juice them. Make the perfect lemonade!

15.
Peel a head of garlic instantly.

How long does it take you to peel an entire head of garlic? Sometimes, I don't even cook with garlic because it takes too long. However, if you place the head of garlic inside of a bowl or a basket and shake it REALLY REALLY HARD, you can peel the head of garlic easily in the following minutes. Seriously. It works.

16.
Make "French fries" with an apple slicer.

You can easily make long strips of potatoes with an apple slicer. Apples and potatoes are very, very similar in their texture. Therefore, when you use the apple slicer on them, it works perfectly to deliver French fry-sized potatoes.

17.
Peel your potatoes in an instant.

It takes a really, really long time to peel potatoes. However, if you already are planning on boiling the potatoes—you don't ever need to peel the potatoes. Instead, simply allow them to boil with their skins on for about 30 minutes. Next, place the potatoes in a bowl of ice water. You can twist the skins away from the potatoes easily.

18.
Slice meat easily with this DIY hack.

Meat can be pretty tricky to slice. However, if you first freeze meat before you cook it, you can slice it easily into its stew and stir-fry slices. Place it in the freezer for a few days. It will retain all its natural freshness, anyway.

19.
Take out cherry pits in a flash.

You can easily remove cherry pits with this hack. First, completely cleanse a paperclip. Then, dig into the cherry with the round end of the paperclip and simply scoop out the cherry pit. This allows you to prepare your cherries before sticking them in your mouth—which is always a hassle!

20.
Make "whipped" cream easily.

Save your elbows some work with this unique hack. Simply bring cream into a Mason jar and then shake the Mason jar as hard as you can. (Note that this IS a lot easier than stirring it with a whisk!) Then, reveal your whipped cream! If you keep going, you can create butter.

21.
Take the peels off a dozen boiled eggs at once.

It can take a long time to peel eggs. However, after you boil your eggs, you should place them all together in a large bowl. Next, you should shake the bowl well, making the shells break up. Next, pour water into the bowl and watch the magic as all of the shells fall off into the bowl!

22.
Remove scattered eggshells from eggs easily.

Whenever you crack an egg and lose a small piece of the shell in the gross gook, it can be pretty difficult to get the small piece out. However, if you make your fingers wet before leafing in there to grab the eggshell, you'll be surprised how easily you can get that thing out. Try it next time!

23.
Make waffle iron hash browns.

It's hard to say why no one has ever thought of this before. But if you just pour your uncooked hash browns into your waffle iron, you can make delightful, super-crunchy hash browns so easily, it's ridiculous.

24.
Open a candy kiss the right way.

Do you usually unwrap your chocolate kisses like they're presents? You're doing it the wrong way! Chocolate kisses were made with ease in mind, but no one uses them correctly. Simply squeeze the end of the wrapper, toward the bottom, and then pull at the "kiss" paper dripping out the top. When you do this at the same time, the wrapping will fall off instantly.

25.
Make instant cheese bread.

Next time you want to make cheesy bread—but you don't want to go all-out—you can use this awesome, super-simple hack. After you make (or buy) a nice loaf of bread, simply slice a checkerboard into the top, dipping the knife into the "guts" of the bread. Next, stick pieces of cheese in the gaps between the pieces of bread. Place the bread in the oven for about five minutes—long enough for the bread to crisp and the cheese to melt—and enjoy!

26.
Make an omelet on a panini maker.

If you like using panini makers and haven't mastered the omelet flip yet, you can use this awesome hack to better your omelets. Simply mix up your eggs and pour the egg batter out onto the panini maker. After it solidifies, place the ingredients you want inside the omelet overtop. Next, fold up the omelet as you please. You'll notice the omelet is not very pretty. But it gets the job done.

27.
Make pancake pops with spare "sucker" straws.

If you want some easy-dipping pancakes, you can make unique pancake pops with this awesome hack. Simply mix up the pancake batter. Next, lay out several sucker straws over a hot griddle. Pour the pancake batter in a circle over the top of each sucker straw. After the batter solidifies over one side, you can flip the pancakes using the straws. Enjoy dipping these pancakes into syrups, etc.!

28.
Create "milk and cookie" ice cubes or the perfect chocolate drink.

This hack is essential for the holiday season. Simply crush several cookies onto a plate. Next, add the cookies to the bottom of an empty ice tray. Pour the milk on top of the cookies, and then place them in a freezer to allow them to freeze. Enjoy them in chocolate milk!

29.
Make your salads easily inside of a jar.

Use this awesome hack to create grab-and-go salads for your at-work meal. Simply portion chickpeas, radishes, edamame, and cucumbers at the bottom of your jar along with some dressing. Next, add the lighter things like your mandarin oranges, mushrooms, corn, onions, etc. Next, add the really light stuff, like spinach, or lettuce. That way, when you pour out the salad into a bowl, everything's in the right order!

30.
Know what to do with asparagus.

When you cook asparagus, you have to understand that you cannot boil the stuff. It will completely render itself useless in flavor and nutrients. You can steam it for 10 minutes or microwave it for four minutes. Don't do anything else!

31.
Make pancakes with cookie cutters.

Next time you make pancakes, why not liven them up a little bit with cookie cutters? Simply place the cookie cutters on the hot skillet and then pour the batter inside the cookie cutters, allowing them to take form. Before you flip them, take the cookie cutter out. The pancakes will have retained their shape!

32.
Make fun eggs the same exact way.

Not as readily thought of, you can actually brighten your eggs with the same pancake hack as above. Simply place your cookie cutters inside of your skillet and then crack your eggs into the cookie cutters. Allow the eggs to solidify before removing the cookie cutters and flipping the eggs. Just don't break the yolks!

33.
Eat a cupcake the right way.

Do you usually eat the frosting first and then lose your love for the bottom part very quickly? Use this hack to eat cupcakes the right way! Simply slice the cupcake horizontally in the middle of the cake part. Then, put the bottom on top of the frosting to make a sandwich. Delicious!

34.
Boil oatmeal water in your Keurig.

If you're running late but you want your oatmeal water STAT, you can simply place your oatmeal bowl beneath your Keurig and let the little guy do all the work for you. Thanks, Keurig! This way, you don't have to put the water on and all that jazz.

35.
Make an "egg" burger.

This is a delightful hack. Listen up. So you create a burger patty. And then, you stab the center of the burger patty with the top edge of a cup, making a round, empty center. Place the burger patty on a skillet and crack the egg in the hole. Then, you cook the egg and the burger meat together, flipping accordingly. Serious. It's so awesome.

36.
Seal your bags with your own CO_2 and keep your food fresh.

If you want to keep vegetables fresh, use this awesome hack. Simply put your vegetables into a plastic bag and blow into the bag. Then, seal the bag really tightly. The CO_2 in your breath will keep the vegetables from wilting.

37.
Place your ice cream cartons inside of zip-lock bags.

Wow. You know how hard your ice cream gets inside of the container? It doesn't have to be that way. We've been living wrong for years! Instead, simply position your cartons inside a zip-lock bag and place the entire bag in the freezer. This way, the ice cream will stay nice and "new-like."

Conclusion:

365 Days of DIY brings you essential household hacks, parenting hacks, cleaning hacks, beauty hacks, ease-your-life hacks, fitness hacks, and, of course, cleaning hacks. From these past 365 days, you have learned a lot. You've learned that you've been wasting your time in previous years. You've been spending far too much time cleaning, working, cooking—etc. There are only so many hours in a day and days in a year. Maximize your time and energy. Fuel creativity in every element of your life. Utilize these DIY hacks and fuel yourself with better understanding of the way your life should work. Today.

Made in the USA
Coppell, TX
17 May 2021